Letters and
Remembrances
from the
Vietnam Veterans
Memorial

SHRAPNEL
IN THE HEART

LAURA PALMER

Random House
New York

Grateful acknowledgment is made to the following for permission to reprint previously published material:

Charlie King: Excerpt from the lyrics to "Trying To Find A Way Home" by Charlie King. Copyright © 1983 Charlie King/Pied ASP Music (BMI), 158 Cliff Street, Norwich, CT 06360. ℗ 1984 Flying Fish Recording, MY HEART KEEPS SNEAKIN' UP ON MY HEAD, FF 347.

W. W. Norton & Company, Inc: The excerpt from a letter from Phil Woodall to his father, from *Dear America: Letters Home from Vietnam*, edited by Bernard Edelman for The New York Vietnam Veterans Memorial Commission, is reprinted by permission of Phil Woodall and the publisher, W. W. Norton & Company, Inc. Copyright © 1985 by The New York Vietnam Veterans Memorial Commission.

Library of Congress Cataloging-in-Publication Data

Palmer, Laura.
Shrapnel in the heart.

1. Vietnam Veterans Memorial (Washington, D.C.)
2. American letters. 3. Vietnamese Conflict,
1961–1975—Biography. 4. Washington (D.C.)—
Buildings, structures, etc.. I. Title.
F203.4.V54P35   1987   959.704'38   87-42652
ISBN 0-394-56027-2

Manufactured in the United States of America

9 8 7 6 5 4 3

Title page photograph by John Campbell

Book design by Carole Lowenstein

*This book is dedicated to those
who never made it home from Vietnam,
both the living and the dead,
and to the people who love them
so very, very much*

Few had forebodings of their destiny. At the halts they lay in the long wet grass and gossiped, enormously at ease. The whistle blew. They jumped for their equipment. The little gray figure of the colonel far ahead waved its stick. Hump your pack and get a move on. The next hour, man, will bring you three miles nearer to your death. Your life and your death are nothing to these fields—nothing, no more than it is to the man planning the next attack at G.H.Q. You are not even a pawn. Your death will not prevent future wars, will not make the world safe for your children. Your death means no more than if you had died in your bed, full of years and respectability, having begotten a tribe of young. Yet by your courage in tribulation, by your cheerfulness before the dirty devices of this world, you have won the love of those who have watched you. All we remember is your living face, and that we loved you for being of our clay and our spirit.

—GUY CHAPMAN, *A Passionate Prodigality*

Magnicourt-sur-Canche, France
21 October 1916

For we do not want you to be ignorant, brethren, of the affliction we experienced in Asia; for we were so utterly, unbearably crushed that we despaired of life itself. Why, we felt that we had received the sentence of death; but that was to make us rely not on ourselves but on God who raises the dead; he delivered us from so deadly a peril, and he will deliver us; on him we have set our hope that he will deliver us again. You also must help us by prayer, so that many will give thanks on our behalf . . .

—2 CORINTHIANS 1: 8–11

Contents

They were ours.

In the simplicity of those three words is the power of the Vietnam Veterans Memorial and the purpose of this book. The memorial asks that you remember; here are their names. *Shrapnel in the Heart* lets you listen; here are their stories, told by the people who loved them.

We have heard about Vietnam from the generals and journalists, soldiers and spies, politicians and historians. Now it is the turn of the people who lost the most and have said the least: the mothers and fathers, sisters and brothers, children, friends, wives, sweethearts, and buddies of the men who died in Vietnam. They tell tenderly, painfully, and sometimes angrily about what it means to lose someone you love in a war that much of the country came to hate. But this is not a book about despair. This is a book about love, love that bombs can't shatter and bullets can't kill.

Shrapnel in the Heart is a collection of letters and poems that have been left at the Vietnam Veterans Memorial in Washington, D.C. In the five years of its existence, the memorial, unexpectedly, became a place not only to honor but to communicate with the dead. The messages that have been left there speak eloquently of loss and remembrance:

"I have dreamed of the day you'll come home and finally be my Dad. You would have been the best Daddy in the whole world."

"I'm the one who rocked him as a baby."

"My prayer, my dear and sweet husband, is that the world would forever know peace."

"Hi Lover! Seventeen years . . . you're still twenty-one—forever young, but gone. Murdered. And nothing will make your loss to us less of a tragedy."

Material like this does not exist at any other American monument. Never before, it seems, have people unburdened themselves on paper and left their intimate thoughts at a public memorial.

When I went to the memorial for the first time, on New Year's Day, 1986, I had no inkling this book was in the offing. I went alone and spent six hours at the wall, mesmerized and moved. The names seemed to go on forever; it felt eternally sad.

Vietnam has been a large part of my life. I grew up in the sixties and worked in Saigon as a reporter in the early seventies. But oddly, when I made that initial visit to the memorial, none of that seemed to matter. I was moved simply as a mother. Name one child, your own, and each of the 58,132 names on the wall will break your heart.

I was fascinated by what was happening at the memorial: one by one, without anyone suggesting it, people were silently crossing over their moat of grief and leaving a letter, poem, or other offering at the wall. It seemed almost un-American; we are so proud, so noisy, so extroverted. Yet here, in a sacred and silent ritual, a side of ourselves that we are reluctant to show was being revealed.

This rite of remembrance began with the plunk of a Purple Heart into wet cement. As the foundation of the memorial was being poured, a man asked construction workers if he could drop his brother's medal into the concrete. He saluted as it slid beneath the surface. There have been more than six thousand similar salutes since the memorial was officially dedicated on Veterans Day, November 11, 1982.

It was then that America finally turned to embrace her own. Engraved on the wall's black granite panels that pry open the earth are the names of every man and woman who went to Vietnam and never came back. In dedicating the memorial, America finally acknowledged that we lost more than the war in Vietnam; we lost the warriors. The war was deplorable, not the men who served. But that distinction—that the outcome of the war was not the fault of the men who fought it—had never been adequately made before. It had been nearly a decade since the fall of Saigon, but the most powerful nation in the world was finally able to say, "They were ours," and begin a long-overdue period of national mourning.

Since then, the Vietnam Veterans Memorial has become the place where America is coming to terms with the Vietnam War. *Shrapnel in the Heart* is a log of part of the journey.

This book was researched, reported, and written during 1986. All of the letters and objects that are left at the memorial are saved by the National Park Service for preservation as part of an eventual museum collection. With determination, luck, and the help of librarians, priests, barbers, high schools, post offices, newspapers, historical societies, and long-distance operators, it is often possible to trace people who have left things there. This is what I set out to do. I wanted to know what motivated people to express their private thoughts in a public place, and how the loss of someone they loved altered their lives, relationships, and aspirations.

As I zigzagged across America, I felt the blistering heat of Kansas in the summer and ate fried catfish and hush puppies at a backyard barbecue in Texas. I saw the leaves turn in New Hampshire and the hunting season begin in Wisconsin. I interviewed a woman by a river in Oregon and another in a beachfront bungalow by the Pacific. I had lobster rolls on Cape Cod and sat down to Sunday dinner with Baptists in the backwoods of Mississippi. I went fishing in an Alabama pond. I looked at scrapbooks in Virginia and stood silently in a small Michigan cemetery. I listened to taped interviews from the Philippines and Japan. In Oklahoma City, I sat in the living room with a family of five as they all cried. A suburb in Los Angeles, a kitchen in Minnesota, a mobile home, a country club—the settings changed but the sadness stayed the same.

Isn't it depressing? was the question my friends asked most frequently during my research. The answer was and remains an emphatic no. It was never depressing because people were grateful for a chance to tell their stories. Sequestered so long with grief, each survivor seemed to think he or she was the only one who continued to mourn so deeply. Time after time, I saw smiles of relief when I told someone about someone else I'd interviewed whose sadness remained intense, even after fifteen or twenty years.

People, I found, not only want to talk about the person they lost in Vietnam, they need to talk. It is a deep yearning in many, suppressed because of the wildly erroneous notion that by now they should be "over it."

The people I interviewed have been given a lot of well-intentioned but bad advice. "Put it behind you, go on with your life." "He was only your brother." "You're young, you'll get married again." "Maybe you are better off," one mother was told. "What if he came home crazy, crippled, or maimed?" Such suggestions only sealed the sorrow deeper inside. I was startled to see that some people felt apologetic, almost guilty, for having so much to tell.

Shrapnel in the Heart is about breaking the silence. Nothing I can write, no story I can tell, will erase anyone's pain, but it can, I hope, crack the isolation which is the tyranny of grief.

Grief, I learned while writing this book, is as individual as a fingerprint. A mother kisses her son's picture every night before she goes to bed; another continues to carry his last letter in her wallet because it is the last thing of his she can touch. Another mother finds solace in writing to her son in the quiet hours after dawn. A father wears his son's Rolex watch. Parents keep his bedroom just the same.

I think the controversy over the Vietnam War stifled a lot of grief. The shame society felt over Vietnam delayed for years any national recognition for the men and women who served there. America's shame, confusion, and humiliation certainly did not dent the pride or love families felt for their sons, but it did lessen the likelihood of their talking about it.

The bitterness surrounding Vietnam stripped it of any honor, and the veterans who did come home were stripped of their dignity. They were ignored if they were lucky, scorned if they were not. And if you lost someone you loved in the convulsion of Vietnam, the way to protect his memory was not to talk about it. As Eleanor Wimbish, a mother I interviewed, said, "I could find people to share my grief because I lost my son, but few wanted to hear where he died."

The soldiers who served in Vietnam were the youngest ever to leave our shores. They fought, and died, at an average age of nineteen, seven years younger than their counterparts in World War II. I always winced when a mother told me her son had never spent a night away from home until he went into the service. These young men became the unwitting pallbearers of America's only military defeat, and it was years before they were forgiven for it.

Courage is the common thread that runs through these stories. *Shrapnel in the Heart* brought me, quite literally, to the doorsteps of the quietly courageous. I have always been struck by the savagery and randomness of the blows that lacerate some lives. I am in awe of the courage it takes to go on.

Rarely do we notice the triumphs that are forged by putting one foot in front of the other, one day at a time. Did we ever really notice that each bullet that took a life in Vietnam stopped several other lives here dead in their tracks? The flag on the coffin covered only the obvious tragedy.

It wasn't just the bodies that were buried, it was the dreams. "I was supposed to marry Joey Sintoni in 1969," remembers Angela Matthews. "I didn't find it easy to progress to Plan B. Marriage was killed in action."

When I began the research for this book, I expected to encounter people who would be unable to talk about the person they loved who died in Vietnam. I thought these people would most likely be mothers, but I was wrong. They were the brothers and sisters. I think their trauma is the least expressed. I think siblings are the least understood victims of the Vietnam War.

Their own needs were underestimated in the avalanche of emotion that descended on their families. Society expects mothers to fall apart and grieve. At least initially, there is a lot of support for a woman who loses a child. But brothers and sisters are told they have their whole life ahead of them. They do not always get a chance to grieve adequately for the part of their life that is behind.

I think the grief of siblings was often internalized because they didn't want to burden anyone else. Sometimes it was discounted completely. No one put it more vividly than Yvonne Sherman, who remembers people responding to her news of losing a brother in Vietnam by saying, "Oh, I feel so sorry for your mom and dad." Difficult, too, was measuring up to a brother who became perfected in death.

Time occasionally makes loss more bearable. But for siblings, their own passage through life can be a jarring reminder of just how much their brother missed. Sally Van Valin summed it up when remembering her youngest brother, David Stoll. "I always thought someday we would be grown up and visit each other with kids and play cards in the evening, and it just hasn't turned out that way. I miss him, all the things that might have been, and finding out what he would have been like as a grown-up person. I would have loved to see how he would have held a baby and taken care of a child of his own."

I also believe that the ideal of the strong, silent man is still very much with us. Fathers. One of the saddest things I heard while interviewing was the comment of a women who said she had never seen her husband cry about their son's death. "But sometimes he'll go out in the garage and spend a couple of hours there and he'll come back and his eyes will be all red and I know he's been crying."

While reading through the hundreds of letters and poems that have been left at the memorial, I never encountered one that was written from a father to his son. Sometimes a man would write "Love, Dad" on the bottom of a note from his wife, but rarely was there anything more. Fathers who were home when I arrived participated in the interviews with eagerness and candor, but they are apparently less inclined to express themselves in writing.

Minorities are also severely underrepresented among the traceable letters left at the wall. When I began this book, I was certain that some of the letters would turn out to have been written by blacks. Only one did, and the writer, through a friend of her brother's, declined to be interviewed. I was never able to speak with her directly. My dilemma was that my work was defined not by what I sought, but by what I was able to find.

It may well be that blacks leave material anonymously; black vets may be more likely to leave a medal or other object than a letter. So far, the lack of letters from blacks remains a mystery to me. What is undeniable are the simple facts of Vietnam: in the first fully integrated war, blacks fought as ably and nobly as any other soldiers. In fact, in some years they gave more; for example, from 1965 to 1967, blacks represented only 11 percent of the U.S. population but roughly 23 percent of the war's combat casualties. (However, by the end of the war blacks represented only 12.5 percent of the total killed in the Vietnam War.) Those who survived came home and found their service in Vietnam was one more reason for discrimination in America.

Women also made enormous contributions and sacrifices in Vietnam, something that has until recently been forgotten by everyone and hidden by many of the women themselves. An Army nurse who did just that tells why in this book.

Everything that is left at the memorial is being processed by MARS, the Museum and Archeological Regional Storage facility. Each item that arrives at the warehouse is dated and tagged and carefully preserved in metal cabinets with cushioned drawers. Seeing the material for the first time is like wading through emotional debris hurled to the surface years after a terrible shipwreck.

Throughout my research I was surprised by not only the amount but the richness of the poetry that is left at the memorial. I wondered why people who may have had little exposure to poetry chose it as a way to express their feelings. The best explanation for this phenomenon came from a Vietnam vet in Wichita, Kansas, Rick Rogers, who told me, "When you've been to the abyss and stared into the pit of hell, you look for the opposite to explain it, sort of like yin and yang."

Veterans leave many of the mementos. There are dog tags and dilapidated combat boots, boonie hats and helmets, ragged sweatbands and medals of all kinds, including the Congressional Medal of Honor. Except for a few knives, no weapons have been left at the wall.

The array of objects is eclectic: a can of Vermont maple syrup and seventy-one cents in change. A blue high heel, a Viet Cong wedding ring. There are Bibles and bumper stickers, Buddhas and Saint Christopher medals and a book of Jewish prayers for the dead. There is an eighty-nine-cent shot glass with lyrics from a Billy Joel song tucked inside: "Remember Charlie, remember Baker, they left their childhood on every acre."

There are several teddy bears and scores of flags with messages printed neatly in the red or white stripes. On a dollar bill is written, "A debt so long unpaid, and the beer I promised." There are drawers full of POW/MIA bracelets and cans of C-rations. Someone has left a faded orange wallet-sized calendar with the days crossed off and "Kathi and Bobby" and "Bobby and Kathi" written inside ballpoint hearts. There is an eight-track Carpenters' tape and a can of sardines. A three of spades and a pack of Luckies have been left along with a bicycle-tire tube and a Golden Melody harmonica. Someone left a small Ziploc bag filled with dirt and someone else left seven LOVE stamps in a long white envelope. "Please Write" was scrawled across the front.

The hundreds of snapshots that have been left at the wall form an Instamatic history of the Vietnam War. Some are hideous—disemboweled enemy soldiers. Most are poignant—smiling bare-chested GIs, their arms slung nonchalantly around one another's shoulders. They lean against sandbagged bunkers in lonely-looking places. You think, They look like kids, and then you realize they were.

Two months after my first visit to the memorial, I went to MARS to work on a magazine article. I spent hours alone, reading, thinking, and sometimes weeping. The temperature is deliberately kept cool, for preservation, and it is quiet; only a few people work there full time. That cold and silent backdrop creates an eeriness so palpable it gets you by the throat. Each time I've gone there, I've wanted to flee, but I felt compelled to read, to listen. I had tapped into a gigantic reservoir of pain and I wanted to find out what it meant. How could a memorial elicit such a staggering response?

It happened, I believe, because there was a staggering need. Vietnam isn't behind us at all; it's in us. Sometimes it is only a shard of memory; sometimes it is a ferocious trauma. It defined one generation and influenced those that preceded and followed. To understand it, we need to think about it and feel it; the memorial is the one place we have in common where those feelings can be expressed.

Until we go there, we are, in a sense, incomplete, and so is the memorial.

Maya Ying Lin, the architect who designed the Vietnam Veterans Memorial when she was a twenty-year-old student at Yale, says she never thought of it as V-shaped. She always conceptualized it as a circle to be completed by the thoughts and feelings people bring.

She describes it as the boundary between the living and the dead. We cannot enter their world, but we can peer into it; that is why the memorial is black. In a city of towering alabaster monuments, hers is receding and dark. "White is like a wall, a barrier; it shuts the door. I found black a soothing, deep, deep color because you can look into it forever." She knew not only that the memorial had to be black but that it had to be granite, because granite, when polished, is deeply reflective. When you look at the wall, you see yourself reflected behind the names of the dead. Clouds move, kites fly, trees sway in the reflection behind the names. It is a way of saying that once we can confront and go beyond death, we find renewed life.

This is the essence of healing. Maya Lin understood that it begins with the confrontation of the past and the finding, facing, and touching of a name. So she made her memorial into a journey. One begins by looking up a name in a directory. Then one walks along to a specific panel and finds a specific line; on that line is a name. Because the memorial is arranged chronologically, the name is grouped with others killed on that same day, in alphabetical order. Maya Lin felt that if people could go back and face the traumatic moment in their past, they would be able to go forward again. As she points out, "When you leave the memorial, you have to walk back up into the light. You must choose to do it, to go beyond. To me, it is very much a journey. You have to walk out and leave it in the end."

Her vision originated as a class project at Yale, which earned her a B. She was talked into entering it in the national competition to pick a design for the Vietnam Veterans Memorial, although she was sure she had no chance of winning. But out of the 1,421 entries, hers was ultimately the unanimous choice of a panel of prominent judges. The designers' identities had been kept secret until a winner was selected. When the judges discovered that the architect who was about to rocket into national prominence was a Chinese-American woman who lived in a university dorm, they were shocked.

And so was Jan Scruggs, the grunt-turned-graduate-student who had conceived the idea of building a memorial to his dead buddies. One night after midnight he was sitting alone in his Maryland kitchen drinking scotch. He had been to see *The Deer Hunter*, a gritty, violent film about a Vietnam vet. His mind flashed back to the most disturbing moment of his tour in Vietnam.

On January 21, 1970, twelve of Jan's friends were blown apart while they were unloading an ammunition truck. His eyes fill with tears as he tells the story. Before he changes the subject, he describes how helpless he felt, wandering among the lifeless forms. He tells about seeing a friend with his brains spilling out of his head. When it gets too terrible, he stops.

That night in his kitchen he vowed that he would build a monument in Washington, D.C., with all the names on it. In the coming months, a national fund-raising campaign was organized by Scruggs and Jack Wheeler, Bob Doubek, and Sandie Fauriol. In two years, they would raise nearly ten million dollars, all of it from private contributions.

No one involved with the creation of the Vietnam Veterans Memorial had any idea of how significant it would become. Jan Scruggs thought it would initially attract thousands of visitors but then would turn into just another pretty place to play Frisbee on the Mall. No one anticipated that nearly twenty million Americans would visit it during its first five years.

Vietnam has always been my teacher. I was twenty-two years old when I went there two months after graduating from college in 1972. I went with all the answers and left with only questions. Saigon feels like my hometown because it is where the rest of my life began. It is where I first worked as a reporter and where I wrote the first article I ever published. More important, it is where I met friends I would love forever.

The reporters I know who worked in Vietnam would go back in an instant if it were possible. Rarely is life so passionate and intense as it is when played out against a backdrop of war. Everything matters in a way it never has before, and with constant reminders of death, life becomes both precious and precarious. The only people who really understand that are the people with you at the time. In a war you experience mankind at its worst and at its best. It is a terror and a blessing that you would never trade.

I returned to Vietnam in April 1975, when the country was spinning out of control. It had become harder to stay away than to go back, and so for six hundred dollars I bought a round-trip youth-fare ticket from Paris to Saigon. During my first two years there I had been a radio reporter. During the last month I wrote for a magazine.

I remember the fortune-teller who confided to me her despair. She and her husband had plans to poison themselves and the children if there was a Communist takeover. I wanted to know if her clairvoyance was making her distraught. "Oh, no," she said. "There are some events that overwhelm destiny." It was the best description I ever heard of the Vietnam War.

On April 29, 1975, I left Saigon for the last time, yanked straight up into the sky by a helicopter from a city I had come to love. Tanks rolled into town the next day and the government of South Vietnam surrendered. Saigon was renamed Ho Chi Minh City, but I have never been able to call it that.

Vietnam became my teacher once again in 1986. I traveled thousands of miles, knocking on strangers' doors to ask them about the biggest loss of their lives. It was not always easy.

Yet I will always think of *Shrapnel in the Heart* as a blessing. At times, it seemed to extract a terrible emotional toll from me and from the people I interviewed; we were caught in a riptide of sadness. But I know now that this book gave back more than it took. It gave me the steadying reminder that the legacies of our lives are written in the hearts of those we love.

When I began this book, I thought I was writing about dead soldiers. I finish with the knowledge that they are, spiritually, very much alive.

I don't know if their deaths were a waste, but I know most assuredly that their lives were not. They mattered passionately to the people who loved them, and that has never changed. Their deaths caused wrenching, unending pain and despair. But the magnitude of the pain leads to an understanding of just how much these men were loved. It is by peering through the wretched gloom of their deaths that we see the magnificence of the love that still binds them to the living. Sadly, it is not a love that can stop war, but it is one that defeats death.

The Vietnam Veterans Memorial enabled a nation to say, "They were ours." This book offers the simple rejoinder "Yes, and he was mine."

SHRAPNEL IN THE HEART

EDDIE LYNN LANCASTER

Private First Class, Company F, 3rd Marine Regiment,
3rd Marine Division
AUGUST 20, 1948–DECEMBER 19, 1967

Dearest Eddie Lynn,
I'd give anything to have you shell just one more pecan for me on Grandma's porch.

All my love,
Your cousin
Anne

———•———

W HAT WOULD I SAY to Eddie Lynn if I had one more thought to pass on to him before he died? What are you going to say to a person to make them know that you love them, that you wish they had not had to go through this?

"The only thing I could think of was my childhood and my memories of Eddie Lynn in happier times, when we were all kids and our lives were ahead of us and we were so full of hope and promise for tomorrow. I thought of the most enjoyable thing he and I had ever done together, and that was sitting there eating those pecans out of my grandmother's pecan trees. They were good, oh, they were good."

Anne Pearson is Eddie Lynn's cousin. They were especially close because he had no brothers or sisters. When he was a toddler his mother had divorced his father and moved back into her parents' small house with the big porch in Sour Lake, Texas. Anne's family came frequently on weekends, and she and her brother and sister took the place of the siblings Eddie Lynn never had.

"The smells of Sour Lake were very distinct. The grounds around my grandma's house were mostly woods and the leaves that fell on the ground were never raked—no reason to. Consequently, the leaves would rot, and new leaves would fall. In the heat and humidity of the Texas Gulf Coast, these rotting leaves had a distinct odor. It was not unpleasant—smelled much like a package of potting soil smells when you first open it—maybe a little greener than that. Even today, if you live close to the woods, the smell is everywhere."

Every November, when the trees were laden with pecans, the children would gather them up by the handful. "Of course you didn't dare peel them in the house. You always had to sit on the porch. This was before everybody had TV sets, and in the South, your social life centered around the porch. It always had an overhang, and you could sit out there in the worst rainstorm and not get wet. You could sit out there and be cool, and in the evening, neighbors would come over and talk about the day's activities."

The children would open the pecans with a nutcracker or split them with a brick or a hammer. Eddie Lynn's grandfather had mastered the art of extracting the pecans in perfect halves, which he would sell to neighbors. The ones the family kept were used for pies (made with ribbon cane sugar), Christmas candies, and cakes.

"We would have big Sunday dinners at my grandma's house," Anne continues. "Fried chicken, ham, roast beef, mainly the sort of thing that will cook for a couple of hours while the family goes to church." Later in the afternoon, it would be time for Anne's family to drive home. "It seemed like every time we would leave to go home, Eddie Lynn would be standing on the porch waving goodbye. I can remember my mother saying, every time, 'Poor Eddie Lynn.' And to a southerner, there's a lot of love and affection and sympathy in those words, just 'Poor Eddie Lynn.' I remember when I got the phone call that he died, that was the first thought that went through my mind, Poor Eddie Lynn. It was so devastating to think of that young life being snuffed out."

Eddie Lynn Lancaster was nineteen years old when he stepped on a land mine his third day in Vietnam. It was the week before Christmas; Eddie Lynn's mother hasn't had a Christmas tree since. Hiking through the woods and chopping down a tree was one of the things they had always done together.

Eddie Lynn's mother, Betty Beimbrink, pronounces his name softly as a two-syllable word, EdLynn. "When I think of Eddie Lynn, the main thing I think of is when he wanted me to do something for him, he'd say, 'Mama, would you do me a favor?' I knew then that he was fixin' to put the touch to me."

He wasn't interested in sports, scouting, or band. He loved to be in the woods, with his dogs. He liked to hunt. "I've got his old hunting horn hanging up there with his dog tags. You call your dogs with it, kind of like Daniel Boone." He'd come home with squirrels, birds, and rabbits—mostly squirrels, which his mother would cook, but not eat.

When Eddie Lynn was twelve, his mother remarried and they

moved out of his grandma's house on Merchant Street. Throughout high school he dreamed of joining the Air Force, and his mother promised him that if he kept his grades up and graduated from high school, she would let him go into the service.

One day she came home from work and found Eddie Lynn sitting on the porch with the Marine Corps recruiter. "My heart went *phtt*. This fellow goes up to the school in his dress uniform, not the olive green, and oh, boy, you can imagine. When I was seventeen, if I had seen a Marine in his dress whites, I would have probably dropped my teeth too.

"I said, 'Now, we talked about your going in the Air Force,' and he said, 'Now, Mama, you promised that if I'd bring my grades up, whatever I wanted to do, you'd help me do.' I never made a promise to him I didn't try to keep." She signed the papers, and he joined the Marines.

Boot camp changed him. His mother felt it toughened him up and taught him "that life is not a bowl of cherries." He said he liked the Marine Corps and was very proud to have made private first class.

When he left home again, it was for further training in San Diego. His mother remembers: "I had no idea that was the last time I'd ever see him, but yet, in a way, I knew it. I kind of had a very depressing feeling when he walked across that runway and got on that plane because I knew—no one had ever told me but I knew—he was on his way to Vietnam."

In San Diego, Eddie Lynn's path again crossed that of his cousin Anne. She was in her mid-twenties and was working as a secretary at the Marine base. She had grown up in a conservative household —her father had a career in the Navy—and she never questioned authority or paid much attention to the outside world until John Kennedy was assassinated in 1963.

"I think that one single event started me thinking that all was not right with the world. I had just turned twenty-two when Kennedy was killed, I had a little girl and another baby on the way, and I remember thinking, What kind of world am I bringing these children into? I started paying attention to what was going on, and then I started working on the Marine base in 1966, and all of a sudden, I'm seeing all these young kids coming in for recruit training. The platoons kept getting larger and the training period kept getting shorter and every evening you'd turn on the news and you'd be eating supper and watching Uncle Walter and you'd hear about the body count."

When Eddie Lynn came through as a young recruit, Anne remembers, he seemed happy and enthusiastic. "He kept raving about how much he liked the food in the mess hall. He was so full of life and ready to take on the world."

But he didn't survive his first patrol in Quang Nam province.

"We kept sending our young American boys over there and they would be killed and not come back, but we weren't gaining any ground, and these Vietnamese and Chinese—whoever it was we were fighting over there—we couldn't kill them all. My life wasn't any better because Eddie Lynn and all his peers died. The world that I knew was not any safer. The more we questioned our leaders, it seemed, the more stubborn they got and dug their heels in. I thought, Oh, my God, I've got a little kid four years old—is he going to have to go over there and die?

"Eddie Lynn was only nineteen when he joined the Marines instead of going to college," his cousin remembers, "so his life was not particularly eventful in any way, but he meant a lot to a lot of people, and when he was killed, it brought the Vietnam War closer to our home. It was almost as if someone grabbed us by the shoulders and said, 'Wake up, you fools! Look at what is happening in the world. This young man was one of thousands. They all had mothers, they all had fathers, this was everybody's son.' "

Eddie Lynn's body came home in a sealed casket on New Year's Eve. His mother says: "At first you're kind of numb. You think, This is a dream. I am going to wake up. You drive down the road and you see somebody walking and he walks just like him—he was a long, tall, skinny boy, about six feet two—and your heart goes beating and you think they made a mistake."

Because she never saw his body, there was always hope. When the POWs were released in Hanoi six years after his death, she scanned the columns of names in the newspaper immediately every morning.

The first year after his death, people told her she was spending too much time at Eddie Lynn's grave. "You grieve your way, I'll grieve mine" was all she had to say. Earlier, she and her husband used to go out every Saturday night. "We called it honky-tonking. I loved to dance better than anything. Get a crowd together, go out dancing, have a few drinks, that used to be the meat of life. I wouldn't go dancing now. I haven't gone out at all since Eddie Lynn died."

She lives quietly with her husband in an expanded mobile home not too far from Sour Lake. She is retired and spends her days reading, gardening, watching the hummingbirds at her feeder, and cuddling a Chihuahua named Chloe. "There's very little that actually makes me happy. I can't say I am unhappy, but I don't care like I ought to."

She and her husband have visited the Vietnam Veterans Memorial once. For Betty, who had felt for so long that no one understood how much she suffered, the visit made a difference. "What really impressed me was the number of names. The memorial is, of course, beautiful, but when I looked at those names, I thought, How could I say there was no one who understood how I felt?"

Anne Pearson, Eddie Lynn's cousin, is now the secretary to the commandant of the Marine Corps in Okinawa, Japan. She went to the Vietnam Veterans Memorial for the first time on a sultry August Sunday in 1985, while on home leave.

"When I first walked in and saw this slash in the ground, this gash in the face of the earth, it seemed so symbolic of the hurt and bruises that America felt and endured during the war. I saw what looked to me like miles and miles of names. I started walking into that gash and I started reading those names and the enormity of it just flooded over me. By the time I got to the third or fourth panel, the tears were coming out and I could barely walk."

When she reached Panel 32 East, she had to sit down on the grass. "I was shaking so bad and crying so hard, not just for Eddie Lynn, but for all those names, for all those families." Her friend suggested that she write a note to Eddie Lynn. They had brought paper and pencils with them to make a rubbing. At first, the idea seemed stupid. But then another idea came to her.

"I thought to myself that I'd love to get this load off my mind. I thought if I had one more chance to peel a pecan with Eddie Lynn, he'd still be alive. He'd be in his thirties, have a wife, children, and we could all sit there on Grandma's porch; we'd all be happy again. That's what I wrote on my note, because at that moment I honestly felt that if he could have just one more chance to peel one more pecan, everything would be all right. I was very broken up. So I stuck that little note in the crack by the panel and sat down on the side there on a grassy bank."

Michael,

We grew up together. We served together. You died and I lived. I never could understand that. You were a much better person than me. I'll always remember you.

Life has never been the same without you.

Your buddy,
Tom

Dad,

I came to visit you today. I haven't ever felt so close to you before. I never got a chance to know you but I love you very much. There isn't a day go by Mom doesn't think of you. Me and Gladene are always thinking of you too. You're gone from us now but we'll all be together again one day. You'll never be forgotten, you still live in every one of us. I'm really proud to be your son, I hope I can be as good a man as you were. I love you Dad and I'll be back to see you if its the last thing I ever do.

Your son,
Carwain L. Herrington, USN

JOSEPH E. SINTONI

Specialist Four, Company C, 5th Battalion, 60th Infantry,
9th Infantry Division
NOVEMBER 12, 1945–MARCH 27, 1968

Joseph E. Sintoni

*My dearest friend of all my high school years—my college years.
We grew up together—half-up anyway. I'd hoped we could grow old
together. How little I knew how dependent I was on you. We could
never talk about losing you—the "conflict" was unpopular. But, oh,
how we felt it. Now, these past three years the Nation is coming to
its senses and recognizing what you and your friends of great courage
sacrificed. I knew you to be a man of sensitivity, of honor and full of
a sense of responsibility. You went, you didn't have to go—a
volunteer—a patriot who believed in your country and accepted the
good and the difficult with that belief. I miss you now as much as I
missed you then. Your death changed my life in a way I didn't even
know until just recently. I will always hold you in a special place in
my heart. And you will grow old with me. For you were and always
will be a part of my life and our memories do not dim with the
passing of time. I have told some friends that this trip to
Washington was a pilgrimage. I am coming here to honor you and
the many who gave themselves for their family, friends and country.
We have loved you always and we respect the choices you made.
Perhaps someday we'll meet again.*

Fondest affections,
Angela

———————•———————

HE HAD KISSED Angela Prete for the last time and the good-byes
had all been said. Joe Sintoni boarded a plane and was on his
way to Vietnam. He turned to his diary for company:

*In two minutes, we're in the clouds. How can I describe the feeling of
loneliness and deep loss? Tears appear. I'll not see the familiar faces
and places for 366 days. I go with an ominous feeling. I know that
death may be awaiting me or possibly a maiming wound. But I volunteered to go and my regrets are the hurt I cause my loved ones.*

Joe Sintoni had enlisted in the Army and had been assigned to spend the final eighteen months of his three-year tour as an honor guard at Arlington National Cemetery. His family had been afraid that he might have to go to Vietnam; they were relieved.

It was late 1967. The war was escalating and so were the casualties. Joe Sintoni was part of the final salute: the flag, clean, crisp, and folded fast; the solitary bugle; the silent mothers, fathers, widows, children. Joe stood at attention on the sidelines.

Why them and not me? was the thought that started going through his head. Why not me? These were men his own age. While they had been fighting and dying for freedom, he had been protected and safe. Joe was a patriotic young man who had grown up on Cape Cod. He believed that if you love your country, you are obligated to defend it, and he was determined to do his part. He didn't want to die, but he could not continue to stand idly by at Arlington National Cemetery. When he volunteered for Vietnam, his parents were devastated; Angela was the only one who didn't try to stop him.

"I do, and I did then, respect what he felt was important," she says now. "I was only nineteen or twenty, and I was still very much my parents' child. Today, I might have had a more intense discussion with him. But it was just the beginning of 'the revolution' ; it was before a generation of people said, Wait, these things are wrong. I was just a good girl, trying to do the right thing." That year, Angela remembers, the big issue at her college was whether women should be allowed to wear slacks to class.

Angela and Joe had grown up together, their childhoods rooted in the traditions of New England. Their group of friends in the small town of Sagamore, Massachusetts, called themselves the Grape Stompers because most of them came from Italian families.

Angela, in a teenage poem to Joey, set down her memories of their first kiss—memories "of a beautiful moonlit sky, dripping shining stars for the young lovers; of fine sand, cold beneath our feet; of the chilling November evening air, of silver waves gently washing a pebbled shore; of that first kiss while in waters rooted . . ." Angela lost his high school ring that night in the waves at Scusset Beach.

Joe got to Vietnam in January 1968 and was stationed in the Mekong Delta area near the Cambodian border, where carnage was commonplace. This is where he unfurled his patriotism—along with a large American flag that he brought with him from Arlington.

History had been one of Joe's interests in high school and he had read a lot about World War II. Much of his idealism came from the nobility of that cause, and he thought Vietnam was going to be the same kind of war. But he quickly found out it wasn't. As he wrote in his diary:

This was the second lieutenant I've gone through since getting here. Charlie is going wild. He's beating the hell off of us. The reason is that we're getting no replacements and having to fight short-handed which can't be done effectively. We need men so desperately over here it's pathetic. Why should my buddies and me die for nothing when having a few more men would save us? Oh hell, all descriptions of that night can be summed up in one word, massacre.

His company's position had been overrun by two battalions of Viet Cong in a surprise attack.

They were doped up on pot and just came walking in. They had brand new AK-47 rifles, the best weapon in Vietnam. They killed all our wounded. The Viet Cong were so high on pot that they would laugh at you as you shot them.

When morning came, there were twenty-five dead Americans and ninety-five dead Viet Cong.

Joey, the bright-eyed boy of pride and purpose, began to feel doomed. He confessed in his leather diary:

March 2, 1968. A sad day, the worst day for me in the time I've been here. My best friend was killed last night. He was my very best friend. We came together, we were going to go on R and R together. We fought for our lives next to each other, now he is no more. He had been going with his girl for five years and was going to be married the same June as me. Everyone called him "Hoss." Oh, Hoss, please be in heaven, I'm so blue and morose. Earle Althehaus, that was his name. I'll remember him for the rest of my life.

Joe Sintoni had been in Vietnam for almost two months. Of the twelve men in the group he had arrived with, he was the only one still alive or strong enough to fight.

I am not trying to be a fatalist, but I realize I'll never be able to make one year alive in the field, unless the fighting drastically changes or the war ends, both of which are unlikely. The "oldest" guy in my platoon, one still in the field, still able to fight, has been here six and a half months. All of a sudden I realize I may never see the woman or family my heart beats for. I dare not make a friend.

There was a mortar attack the night of that entry and a corporal friend of Joey's was killed. The next day Joe attended a Sunday mass.

It was so refreshing. I received communion and feel renewed. During Mass, I felt in another world. I want to be close to God. Maybe I'm being hypocritical, but I do want for religion, to get back into the fold. I feel close to God because I know I may stand before him.

Two days later, Joe was going back to the field. "I do feel a great fear. . . . When I came here, I didn't have this dread. Things were different. Now I realize that I'm the second oldest man in the field and the oldest will be leaving in two weeks."

Joe knew the implications of that were bad for him. In his unit, the oldest man had to "walk point"—be the scout who went out first to look for land mines, booby traps, and ambushes.

All of my buddies are either dead or wounded. It makes a guy feel funny. I have nine and a half months to go and I really want to go home. So, I'll leave with hopes of being able to continue this diary. I know the prayers of my loved ones are with me.

He made it back to camp and three days later was writing of "the usual hell" in his journal:

There was one incident that made an indelible spot on my mind. The Viet Cong blew up a track [armored personnel carrier]. I've seen very many tracks blown up, but never like this. There were six men on the tracks. One man could be put in five Skippy jars. The largest part found was a man from the waist up. There was one man that couldn't be found. It was complete carnage. I can't describe it except to say I was sick. I'm now the oldest man out there. That means that every man in my two and a third months has been killed or wounded critically enough to be kept from the field. Why do I always write of bad things? I guess because things are so terribly bad.

Nineteen days later, Joe Sintoni was dead. The flag that he had brought from Arlington Cemetery was gone, too. Joe had written about watching the flag burn when the tank it graced was hit by a rocket. Joe said his flag "flew proudly to its hot death."

The news of Joey's death was broken to Angela indirectly. A relative asked if she remembered the Robert Frost poem that ends "And miles to go before I sleep . . ." At first, she didn't get it, but then it hit. Joe was dead.

The whole predictable course of Angela's life had come to an end in Vietnam. She and Joey had already picked out the names for the children who would fill their two-story dream house overlooking the Cape Cod Canal. "I lost that dream. When he died, I just didn't pick up the pieces and go out and find some boyfriend I could marry. It didn't happen that way. I muddled along for the first few years. It was so bizarre. I was supposed to marry Joey Sintoni. I didn't find it easy to progress to Plan B. Marriage was killed in action. I was mourning the loss of Joey Sintoni, and I didn't even think about mourning the loss of marriage and children and all the other things that were given up at the same time."

Eight days after Joe died, Martin Luther King, Jr., was gunned down, and two months later Robert Kennedy was assassinated. Angela's world was on fire. "I had that sense of futility, of what's the use. It took a long time for me to care again and feel hopeful. I think Joe's loss made me forget all the frivolities—the fun of high school, the fun of knowing Joe when we were growing up—because it made me old real fast."

Angela finished college in 1969, then ran away to Europe. She would have kept running if she hadn't become so homesick at Christmas. She came back, got a job, and had many relationships with men who, she says now, were clearly inappropriate for marriage or raising a family.

It was not until she met David, the man who was to become her husband, that she finally began to come to terms with Joe's death. He encouraged her to talk, to cry; he accepted the depth and endurance of her love for Joe. David didn't make fun of the big shopping bag that Angela hauled with her from move to move, a bag filled with every letter she had ever received from Joe and all the mementos of their high school years. As Angela put it, "Those relationships from our adolescence are the most important to us our whole lives. We never let ourselves be that vulnerable again."

Today as Angela Prete Matthews nears forty, she lives in Portsmouth, New Hampshire, a town as picturesque as the ones in travel brochures. For the past eight years she has been the executive director of a day-care center that is considered a model program, and she was recently named one of the state's "Women of the Year."

She went to the Vietnam Veterans Memorial for the first time in May 1985. As she was driving to Washington, D.C., with her mother she thought about writing something for Joe. She had no idea what to expect.

"When I go to the Cape, I can't bring myself to go to Joe's grave. I know I should, but I can't do it. Yet when I go to that monument, I feel that he's there. He really is there. It's such a spiritual experience. There is a presence there of the people we loved. I remember feeling at peace." She took a picture of Joe's name, and when it was developed, she found it also showed her own reflection on the wall.

The day he left for Vietnam, Joe's mother remembers, he spent a lot of time upstairs. She didn't know what he was doing; she found out only after his death. He was writing three letters—to be opened only if he was killed. One was to his parents, one was to his best friend, George, and one was to Angela.

This is what he wrote on January 1, 1968, to the woman he loved most in the world:

Dear Angela,

This is by far the most difficult letter I shall ever write. What makes it so difficult is that you'll be reading it in the unhappy event of my death. You've already learned of my death; I hope the news was broken to you gently. God, Angie, I didn't want to die. I had so much to live for. You were my main reason for living. You're a jewel, a treasure, a woman whose attributes are sought by every man.

You were to be my wife. I thank God for giving me those few happy years with you. Our future was uncertain, but I did have a lot of confidence. No, I didn't want to die, but death was part of my job.

Please don't hate the war because it has taken me. I'm glad and proud that America has found me equal to the task of defending it.

Vietnam isn't a far-off country in a remote corner of the world. It is Sagamore, Brooklyn, Honolulu, or any other part of the world where there are Americans.

Vietnam is a test of the American spirit. I hope I have helped in a little way to pass the test.

The press, the television screen, the magazines are filled with the images of young men burning their draft cards to demonstrate their courage. Their rejection is of the ancient law that a male fights to protect his own people and his own land.

Does it take courage to flaunt the authorities and burn a draft card? Ask the men at Dak To, Con Tien, or Hill 875, they'll tell you how much courage it takes.

Most people never think of their freedom. They never think much about breathing, either, or blood circulating, except when these functions are checked by a doctor. Freedom, like breathing and circulating blood, is part of our being. Why must people take their freedom for granted? Why can't they support the men who are trying to protect their lifeblood, freedom?

Patriotism is more than fighting or dying for ones country. It is participating in its development, its progress and its governmental processes. It is sharing the never fully paid price of the freedom which was bequeathed to us who enjoy it today. Not to squander, not to exploit, but to preserve and enhance for those who will follow after us.

Just as a man will stand by his family be it right or wrong, so will the patriot stand where Stephen Decatur stood when he offered the toast, "Our country, in her intercourse with foreign nations, may she always be in the right, but our country, right or wrong."

We must do the job God set down for us. It's up to every American to fight for the freedom we hold so dear. We must instruct the young in the ways of these great United States. We mustn't let them take these freedoms for granted.

I want you to go on to live a full, rich, productive life. I want you to share your love with someone. You may meet another man and bring up a family. Please bring up your children to be proud Americans. Don't worry about me, honey. God must have a special place for soldiers.

I've died as I've always hoped, protecting what I hold so dear to my heart. We will meet again in the future. We will. I'll be waiting for that day.

I'll be watching over you Angie, and if it's possible to help you in some way, I will.

Feel some relief with the knowledge that you filled my short life with more happiness than most men know in a lifetime.

The inevitable, well, the last one: I love you with all my heart and my love for you will survive into eternity.

Your Joey

Dear Raymond,

We used to write you everyday so it seems natural to sit and write this note. I wanted to bring those undelivered letters; but some things are too difficult to part with. Maybe I should leave Mom some space; so 'till we meet again.

Your ever loving Sis, Adrienne

P.S. Happy New Year, wherever you are

My Dear Raymond,

You are with us all the time. We miss you and our hearts are sad and lonely. Looking forward when we will all be together. We all love you, Mother.

Dear Ray,

Do you remember when you didn't need to use stamps? I can write free now too. Never thought this would be your new address: Panel 22 West, Line 27.

PP.S. My husband Michael is very proud of you too. He only wishes he could have met you.

PPP.S. Daddy is with you
John grew up and Winne got wise

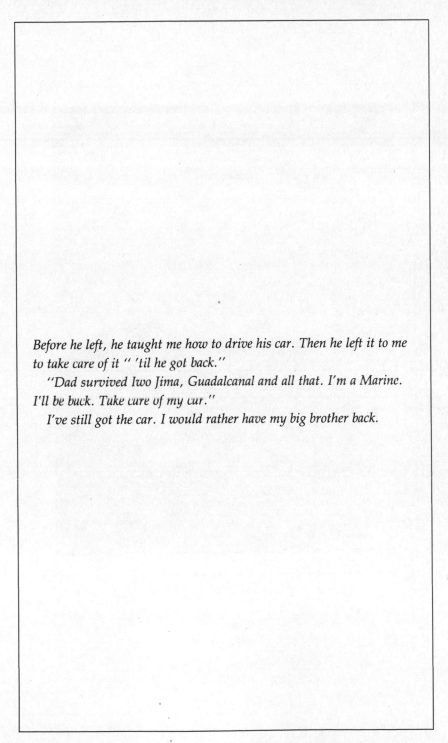

Before he left, he taught me how to drive his car. Then he left it to me to take care of it " 'til he got back."

"Dad survived Iwo Jima, Guadalcanal and all that. I'm a Marine. I'll be back. Take care of my car."

I've still got the car. I would rather have my big brother back.

BERNARD ARTHUR McDERMOTT III

Captain, Company A, 3rd Military Police Battalion,
3rd Marine Division

August 31, 1940–September 6, 1969

My Dearest Ben,

I miss you and think of you so much. Every day in my prayers, I thank God and Jesus for caring for you and pray that will continue. I'm bringing "Teddy Bear" and a picture of your loved race car. I realize they can't stay there long, but they are yours and I want them to be with you. In time, I hope we can all be together.

> *Love to you my dear, dear, Ben*
> *Mama*

Much love,
Dad

———————•———————

SEVENTEEN YEARS after his death, Ben McDermott's Rolex watch still ticks on his father's wrist, his 1964 red Corvette is parked in his best friend's garage, and BoBo, his frayed and fragile teddy bear, is being preserved for history.

"These are things of Ben's that just kind of live on," says his father, a retired Army colonel.

"It seems to me I can still see him in that chair he used to bounce in outside," Ben's mother adds. "He would bounce and bounce and he was always holding BoBo. He always slept with him . . . he called him Boo-Boo."

Ben McDermott was a big, strong, athletic guy who loved motorcycles and fast cars. "If there was going to be action, he wanted to be there," says his father. He played football, parachuted, and had a black belt in karate. He was someone who hurtled through life, and his mother thinks he would want to be remembered as "a brave and fearless person." Yet he had a quiet and gentle side. No matter where he had been, whenever he came home, he always went into the den to say hello to BoBo, who was perched on a shelf.

The McDermotts left BoBo at the base of Panel 18 West on their first visit to the Vietnam Veterans Memorial. Taking the bear to Washington was a spur-of-the-moment decision, made as they were getting ready to leave their home in Nashville, Tennessee. Miriam McDermott remembers that her husband didn't think much of the idea. "You said, 'How silly, how silly,' and I think you didn't want me to belittle Ben by leaving it at the memorial."

Ben's father says now that he was sorry to see the bear go; he had grown attached to it over the years. But he thought maybe some other little boy would pick it up and love it the way Ben had.

The McDermotts think the memorial is "an outstanding way to recognize those who participated in the war." "I was very pleased with it, particularly the black color," says Colonel McDermott. "I've been to many memorials for World War II, and those don't really have the pull that this one does. This one just seems to reach out and bring people in. Most memorials have a cold feeling, but this one doesn't. It has a real warm feeling. . . . When we got there I felt perfectly at home. I felt a great attachment, like we had found him at last."

Ben McDermott never seemed to get enough of the Marine Corps, or of Vietnam. He was on his third tour of duty when he was killed. "He had a dedication to help people in Vietnam. He knew why he was fighting," his father explains. "He would work at a civilian occupation for a couple of months and then back he would go."

On his first tour, in 1965, he was a reconnaissance officer. He was wounded twice and came home, but he turned around and went back again, this time to do a stint for the CIA. His cover was the role of aircraft mechanic. Ben's parents remember his leaving with a toolbox that was part of his getup. He knew nothing about aircraft maintenance, but that didn't matter because shortly after he got to Thailand he was parachuted in behind enemy lines, somewhere along the Ho Chi Minh Trail.

Ben's job was to monitor the enemy troops and supplies that were coming down the pipeline. He worked with five or six Vietnamese, observing and counting the equipment that rolled by. It was a difficult and arduous assignment, but he loved it. His dad has the small journal in which he logged entries for that tour: "killed a centipede twelve inches long"; "arrived at Hill 310, 4 men, bad colds, cloudy rain and fog, decided to sit out the night, spotted many pungi sticks on trail, many felled trees . . . "

Ben ended that tour in 1968, stayed home briefly, and returned in 1969 to Vietnam. Two weeks before his departure he got married. In retrospect, his family was struck by two other things he did before he left for the third time: he gave his dad his Rolex and asked him to keep it until he came home; and he said that if anything happened to him, his shiny red Corvette should go to his best friend, Jimmy McGowan.

Ben's third tour lasted only three weeks. His position near Danang was overrun on September 6, 1969, and he was killed by mortar fire.

Ben and Miriam McDermott will tell you that you never get over the loss of a child, but that time helps you accept the fact of the loss. Colonel McDermott says he knew he was learning to live with Ben's death when he stopped opening the drawer of the circular end table in the living room that contains all of Ben's personal things. It is like a time capsule. Janis Joplin's "Cheap Thrills" album is there, along with Ben's dark leather billfold holding his American Express card and military identification. There are his papers, pens, letters, photos —all the basic props of everyday life.

The McDermotts have made the back porch, the one where Ben used to sleep, into a room of memories and mementos. Ben's saber from the Marines and some of his military emblems are framed and mounted, and so is the flag that draped his coffin. A print of his favorite painting, a Rembrandt portrait of an old soldier, hangs over the television set. A cookie tin holds his snapshots from Vietnam, and his karate belts are beside it on the bookshelf. There's a picture of Ben in his football jersey over the old sofa. "We just kind of dedicated the room to him," says Colonel McDermott. "I don't know if other families do this, but sometimes we kind of feel like he's here."

Colonel McDermott lived and loved the life of a soldier. From 1943 to 1946 he commanded the 290th Combat Engineer Battalion, which normally supplied engineering support to the infantry but was converted to a fighting force in 1945 and battled the Germans in the Vosges Mountains. He and his men still hold annual reunions and keep in touch through a monthly newsletter.

His war was different from his son's. "You didn't have any people that held back, like the ones that left for Canada. They wanted to participate because they knew what the cause was and there was a strong desire to accomplish something. The country was behind it and you knew from the ground swell that it was a worthy cause."

He feels the military in Vietnam was held back by the politicians.

"It was a bigger job than they anticipated, and then the military was in a helpless position. The people that were in charge, like Westmoreland, were very competent. But they never had a chance to exercise their own desires."

Miriam's analysis is much simpler. "My son lost his life because of Vietnam, and it was a useless war."

An open letter to my brothers:

This marks the 2nd year I have come to the wall. I have seen the names of those I know and yes, I have cried. My problem is I don't know the names of those I tried to help only to have them die in my arms. In my sleep, I hear their cries and see their faces.

As a young kid, I was raised around the lakes of Indiana. I used to live for nothing more than spending time boating and swimming, or being around the cool shore line of a lake.

In Vietnam, at age 20, I was put in charge of a river boat. Now every time I get on a boat I only see the red blood running over the deck and into the water. I try to take my 2 sons fishing but we never stay out long. The fish don't seem to bite when I take them out, like they do when they go with someone else's father. They are too young to understand that their father does not like the reflections he sees in the water.

For these reasons, I write to say I'm sorry. I am the third son in three years to serve in Vietnam from my family. Like my brothers before me, I did the best I could. To all you mothers, fathers, brothers, sisters, wives and lovers of these men, I am sorry "I could do no more." I can count the numbers, 113 missions to be exact. My boat was always first, I made sure of that. You know, never send anyone somewhere you wouldn't go yourself.

I wish I knew your names so I could touch your names in the black stone. But I don't and I'm sorry. "So sorry."

Attached to this letter are my service medals. I don't need them to show I was there. I have your faces to remind me in my sleep. I will leave now to return to my safe place. My wife, who has stuck by me for 13 years, and my sons, I will bring them here some day and show them the wall. But we now know I can never show them all the names.

Rest well, my brothers, may the wind be to your backs and the sun in your face. On the day we meet again, please do one thing, "Tell me your name."

Love,
Your brother
Glen

Dear John,

I remember with great fondness our time together, our time for love, sharing. Never in even my wildest dreams did I think we would be stationed so close together.

Those nine months—times of joy and sorrow will stay in my heart forever. Only now, after seventeen years, am I really able to accept the fact that you are no longer here. You will always be in my heart, a part of me forever.

Gone now too are the nightmares reliving the terrible night of your death. How I held you in my arms, your blood soaking through to my skin.

Be peaceful, knowing you died valiantly. I, too, am at peace, knowing at last I can say goodbye.

With love,
M. J.

Dear 'Smitty,

Perhaps, now I can bury you; at least in my soul. Perhaps, now, I won't again see you night after night when the war re-appears and we are once more amidst the myriad hells that Vietnam engulfed us in.

We crept 'point' together and we pulled 'drag' together. We lay crouched in cold mud and were drenched by monsoons. We sweated buckets and endured the heat of dry season. We burnt at least a thousand leeches off one another and went through a gallon of insect repellent a day that the bugs were irresistibly attracted to.

When you were hit, I was your medic all the way, and when I was blown 50 feet by the mortar, you were there first. When I was shaking with malaria, you wiped my brow.

We got tough, 'Smitty. We became hired guns, lean and mean and calloused. And after every ambush, every firefight, every "hot" chopper insertion you'd shake and get sick.

You got a bronze star, a silver star, survived 18 months of one demon hell after another, only to walk into a booby trapped bunker and all of a sudden you had no face or chest.

I never cried. My chest becomes unbearably painful and my throat tightens so I can't even croak, but I haven't cried. I wanted to, just couldn't.

I think I can, today. Damn, I'm crying now.

> *'Bye Smitty,*
> *Get some rest*

ALLAN JOHN DYER

Warrant Officer, Troop A, 7th Squadron,
1st Cavalry (Air Cavalry),
164th Aviation Group
JUNE 20, 1950–JULY 17, 1971

I often sit in luscious meadows of thought,
Absorbed solely with memories of a brother whom I lost.

How I cherish those vivid moments
    when once again we lovingly embrace.
But eventually, reality strikes me
    viciously in the face.
I remember that he is gone, and life
    was the cost.

He earned the Purple Heart and
    Distinguished Flying Cross.
"What an honorable end for a twenty-one
    year old," is the consoling remark.
Satirically, the world mourns the loss.

The sun still rises in the east and sets
    in the west.
My life does not cease; ironically, he was
    "Above the Best."

I have stopped asking why, God,
    because you have not answered.
My pleas for his safety fell on deaf ears.
He endured his hell and finally plunged
    into eternal darkness.

I lay wide-eyed in the stealth of darkness.
The night stretches relentlessly before me; my
    grief overwhelms me.
Knowing he sees me, I desperately scream
    "I love you."
He quietly replies, "Don't grieve for I am
    now in ecstasy."

Another day descends on this
    hemisphere.
Visions and memories of a martyred brother
    are put behind closed doors.

I HAVE CRIED A LOT about Allan, but not where people could see it," Yvonne Sherman says. "People don't really think you can have that close a relationship with your brother. After a while you don't want to bring it up. I'm a very private person anyway."

One response she often heard when she told someone she had lost a brother was "I feel so sorry for your mom and dad." At times she was made to feel "You're married to your husband, not your brother," or "You really should be over this by now." So she kept her grief to herself. Her parents were devastated by Allan's death, and her husband was traveling a lot in those early years, so Yvonne would sit by herself at night and cry after she put her baby to bed.

Yvonne was just thirteen months older than Allan. "I really felt like I had a twin brother. I don't remember playing with other children my first five years. We were it." She and Allan were the only children in the family, and they relied on each other. "My mother was sick a lot when we were growing up—she was in and out of the hospital—and so we really had a bond. We helped each other in school. My father did shift work, so we would be home alone a lot. We didn't care. We were perfectly happy together."

Yvonne remembers the summer her grandparents came from Germany for a visit and she had to sleep in Allan's room on a cot. They would turn the radio up loud and listen to the songs of that summer, such as "Don't Let the Sun Catch You Crying," and talk long past the time they were supposed to be asleep. Yvonne was fourteen and had a boyfriend named Ray, and she remembers confiding in Allan about her new romance.

Her blond, blue-eyed brother "looked like a cherub. He was a daredevil and was always getting hurt as a little kid. He thought he was invincible." He played football and loved to go on fishing and camping trips with his dad, but his passion, as far back as Yvonne can remember, was flying. His grandfather had been a pilot, and the desire to fly seemed to be in Allan's blood.

After a year at the University of Toledo, Allan told his family that he had decided to enlist in the Army and go to warrant officer's school. He would learn to fly helicopters, even if it meant a year in Vietnam. He completed his training and married his high school sweetheart just before he went overseas. "The most vivid thing he ever wrote to me was right after he got over there and had flown his first mission. He said, 'I was scared as hell, I took my first hit today.' " But if the fear ran deeper than that, he kept it to himself. He flew a lot of volunteer missions, and nearly every picture he sent home showed him standing by the choppers he was devoted to.

"I do believe that Allan believed in what he was doing. He was patriotic and for that reason he did fight for his country," Yvonne says. She describes their family as conservative. Their father had been a soldier and met his wife in Germany during World War II, and patriotism was not something that one questioned in the Dyer home. Yvonne was aware of the flower children and hippies, but her life was too sheltered, she says, to be touched by all that. And even though Allan was over there, Vietnam seemed far removed from life in Toledo.

"Here I am in sunny Toledo, tooling down the street, all of us forgetting that these guys are in Vietnam. This is how your life was in those days. You saw it in the news, but you didn't really think about it that much because it was so far away. I never thought that he would be killed. That happened to other people. You block it out of your mind. When he was killed, that's when I realized what was going on."

The first report the Dyers received was that Allan was missing. For three days they kept waiting for news of his rescue. But then an Army officer came to the house, and later a telegram gave more details. "As he banked the aircraft to search the tree line he was subjected to intensive enemy fire. The aircraft spun out of control and crashed. It may be of some comfort to you to know he succumbed immediately to his injuries."

A month after her brother's death, Yvonne and her husband moved to Houston, Texas. She was away from her parents and friends and everything familiar. Her husband, a salesman, had to travel, and she was left at home alone with her baby and her sadness. "I was scared staying in that apartment alone. I cried a lot. I definitely repressed my feelings around other people. Even my husband doesn't know how many times I cried when I was alone with our little baby.

"I'll never be the same. But you do go on."

About eighteen months after Allan's death Yvonne had an experience that helped her. "I don't call it a dream, I call it a vision. It happened in February 1973. I had been thinking about Allan a lot.

My husband was asleep. All of a sudden I woke up and saw this light beaming into the bedroom. It was a beautiful, really bright, white light. I opened up my eyes, I saw it, and I saw a vision of Allan. I saw his little cherub face, round and darling, and he said, 'Yvonne, don't grieve. I am in ecstasy.' The light, I think, is what woke me up. It was unbelievable . . . for someone else, but not for me. I know what I saw." The poem that she would take to Washington years later was written after that vision and tucked away in a scrapbook.

Yvonne and her husband still live in Houston, with their children—two boys, sixteen and nine, and a daughter, thirteen. Yvonne has returned to college now that her children are more independent. Her life is full, and her energy and enthusiasm are appealing. Her husband, Dick, has been sympathetic about the loss of her brother, but her children, she says, sometimes tire of hearing about Allan. "Every Thanksgiving, I make up a prayer and I include something about Allan. The kids give me a glance, they look at me."

When Yvonne went to the Vietnam Veterans Memorial with her family, she took her poem; she had heard that people left things there, and "I guess I had this need to let history know how much I missed him and loved him.

"I didn't want to stay there that long. I was with my family. It is more awesome than I thought it would be. It is like a mass tombstone. It is so massive." She would like to go back to the memorial with her parents, who have never been there. She would like to see it when it is dark. "I think going there at night would be a little better. People wouldn't see you at night and you could really let go.

"I know Allan would never want me to dwell on his death. I had a wonderful brother and I have those memories, and I am very fortunate I had him for the space of time that I did. I loved him dearly, and he loved me, and that you can't take away.

"But it took a big piece of me. It changed me. It definitely did. I feel the loss. I feel like there's a void within my heart because a piece is gone. I would say the shrapnel entered my heart and took a piece of it. First there was a great, writhing pain, like someone took a knife and twisted it, and then a piece broke off and went with Allan. Remember, I told you I don't feel completely whole? Allan has a piece of my heart. It feels like a piece of me left. It really and truly did."

Airborne

My Dear Friends,

It is good to touch your names, your memory, and to visit with you.

I've struggled in your absence. I've been so angry that you left me. I miss you so much!

I've looked for you for so long. I worked for so long to try to figure out some way to save you. I've been afraid to rest, knowing that I had to find and save you, that to rest, to stop looking for you would make your deaths a certainty.

How angry I was to find you here—though I knew that you would be. I've wished so hard that I could have saved you. I would give my life if somehow it would bring you back.

It is only now on my second trip to the monument that I can admit that you, my friends, are gone forever—that I can say your names, call you my friends and speak of your deaths.

I've cried for you so many times. I've been dead for so long trying to keep you alive. If only I could have gotten there first—if only you had waited. I know I could have saved you.

I've carried the anguish of your deaths for so long, but I think I can stop looking for you now. I think I can start living without letting you die.

I will never forget you! You will always be a part of me—part of you lives in me. I will carry your memory forever and I will make people confront that memory—the memory of what was done to us. If I could, I would lead each person in hand past this monument and make them read each name and imagine each life that was cut short.

I promise you, my friends, I will never let them forget the price you paid.

"Singer"

Barnett, my brother of war, our skin was not the same but our hearts were. I've missed you soul brother. Travel in peace. You are in good company with our brothers McFarland and Loyd.

This ten pack is on me. I've come to have one last smooth with you.

November 1986

Twenty-one years ago, July, 1965, a caring, gentle 26 year old pilot left for Southeast Asia—certain that by his service, he was helping one of America's allies fight for their freedom and right to self-determination.

Nineteen and a half years later, a handful of bones, a small section of jawbone and two teeth were returned and positively identified as the only mortal remains of this once tall and proud American.

He rests in peace, at last, in his native soil at Arlington.

Through the beautiful daughter that he never saw—born six months after his death—his artistic talent, his characteristics and his compassion for others live on. Memories of him are forever a part of my heart.

I share this with those of you who come to this hallowed wall of names —remembering, seeking comfort and solace for the losses we all suffered as a result of Vietnam. Know that others share your sorrow and pray for you and those you knew and love who are named here forever on this starkly beautiful memorial.

Touch the names you remember and release the pain in your heart so long held. Commit these Americans to God's care and the guardianship of the three who stand as silent sentries on the hill nearby. Pray that our government leaders will find the courage and strength to act to bring home to America the men who still wait for their homecoming. Pray also that the hearts of the leaders of their captors will be softened to let our people go. How much longer must they wait?

The pathway and the ground at this memorial have been deep-watered by the tears of thousands of Americans who remember and who care. I hope someday soon our tears of sadness will turn to tears of joy and thanksgiving when some of the crosses of the MIAs are changed to stars. God bless you all, especially those who served in Vietnam.
Love and Peace,
Dana Chwan
Tampa, Florida

JAMES C. BARBOUR, JR.

Private First Class, Company A, 3rd Battalion,
506th Infantry, 101st Airborne Division
December 13, 1947–August 27, 1968

My dear Jimmy,

It's time to honor our war dead again, and darling, I could cry my heart out.

You fought a war and died. Part of me died with you. I'm still fighting a war I know I can never win. Trying to live without you. My heart is broken forever.

No one knows how hard it is to love and lose, unless they have gone through it.

I carry you in my mind every minute of my life. I talk to your pictures. Say I love and miss you and want to see you so very, very bad, but darling, pictures can't talk back.

I tend your grave and sit and talk to you, but graves can't talk back. If love and tears could have saved you, you would be here today.

I go on my knees and thank God for the pleasure of having you for 20 years. I thank him over and over for the grandson you gave us.

I thank God every day for my two wonderful sons.

My Jimmy and my Wayne. Mama loves you and will forever keep you in my heart until I see you some sweet day, never to part again.

As I prepare to go to Washington, I know it's you I wish to see, but I'll see your name darling. It means you are not coming home to me. I honor and respect it. My hero, my Jimmy, that means so much to me.

I'm sitting here talking to you tonight the way we used to do, but I can't hold your hand and say "Jimmy, Mom loves you."

I didn't want you to go, but you had a job to do.

Jimmy, I'm so glad I held you in my arms and told you how much I loved you that day at Byrd Airport.

When you came back, they wouldn't even let me touch you, darling. I didn't think that was fair. You are my son and I will never forgive them. I gave birth to you and raised you and I begged so hard just to put my arms around you and kiss you goodbye.

Jimmy, I will say goodnight for this time. I'll be talking to you tomorrow. I will never forget you. Your memories are my treasures. I will never let go of them.

I love you and miss you more and more,

XOXO Mom

IT is the Sunday before Veterans Day, 1986. A letter addressed to "My Jimmy" lies at the base of Panel 34 West. A woman stands before it, screaming, "Oh, Jimmy, if I could only get you down from there and take you home with me. I love you, Jimmy. Mama loves you, Jimmy." Her screams are so terrible, so painful, that no one near her moves. The people who know her are frozen. Finally, a friend walks over to Evelyn Barbour and wraps his arms around her until she is still.

Her son was shot in the chest in Cu Chi and lived for five hours after surgery. "I know he fought with everything he had," she says as she sits at her kitchen table in Richmond, Virginia, drinking cup after cup of decaffeinated coffee and inhaling slowly on long slim cigarettes.

Forty years ago she was told she would never have children. Before she and her husband could adopt a child, she had to have a physical, and that's when she found out she was pregnant. There could not have been a happier woman on the planet in 1947. But shortly after her first son, James C. Barbour, Jr., was born, something happened.

"I was rocking him. I just couldn't do enough for the baby. I wouldn't let anybody keep him and I wouldn't go anywhere I couldn't take him." And then, as she was holding him, she had a vision: a robed figure that "looked like Christ" seemed to stand in front of her and say, "Love him. He will not live to be twenty-one."

It was the only vision she ever had in her life. What made it particularly chilling for her was that in both her own family and her husband's, several first-born children had died before turning twenty-one. Not surprisingly, when Jimmy went to Vietnam at the age of twenty, she felt sick.

"He said, 'Mom, I have a feeling I won't be coming back.' I put my arms around him and said, 'I love you too much for anything to happen to you,' and he said, 'No, while I've got the opportunity, I want to tell you I'm right with God.' He said, 'You've been a wonderful mother to me. I have never heard you say, "Wait a minute, I'll do it after a while, I don't have time." Anything Wayne or me asked, you always did.' "

As he was standing on the steps of the plane, waving good-bye, Evelyn Barbour told her family gathered with her there at Byrd Airport, "You look at him good, 'cause you will never see him alive before he is twenty-one."

"People tell you time heals the heart, but that's not so. That's not so because everything in life, you just wish he was by your side. Everything you do, there's an empty spot."

Evelyn Barbour was born in Atlanta, Georgia, but grew up in Richmond. She left high school and married at seventeen. Her husband, James, has had a career in the Air Force. They have a younger son, Wayne. The Barbours are Baptists.

Their friends used to call the Barbour family the Kissin' Four. "We didn't part that we didn't kiss each other, even if it was just to run to the store." Evelyn's home is a shrine to her children and grandchildren. Pictures fill the walls. "I just had the world in my hands when I had them. And this Jimmy, if he couldn't make you laugh. . . . Jimmy was a comic. He loved everybody and he couldn't see a wrong. He pulled the good out of everybody.

"He loved dancing. He could stand flat on two feet and shake every hair on his head and not pick a foot up. I could put on 'Kansas City' and he'd walk in the door dancing."

The Barbour boys grew up in a home without guns or alcohol. Their parents were determined to forge a real family closeness. One night a week, every week, the four of them went out, sometimes for dinner, other times for bowling or miniature golf. Thursday nights, Jimmy and Wayne did something special with their dad.

Evelyn Barbour says that even when Jimmy was little, he wanted to jump out of airplanes. She has no idea why. Once, when he was three, he jumped from his grandmother's second-floor porch; he didn't walk for eight weeks, but neither his dream nor his legs were permanently damaged.

So when he told his mother that he had decided to join the paratroopers, she wasn't really surprised. He had left high school in the eleventh grade to work as an apprentice land surveyor, and at nineteen he enlisted in the Army and went off to basic training. He loved being a paratrooper and was planning to make the Army a career. Hurtling out of planes was all he had dreamed it would be. He volunteered for Vietnam because he knew that sooner or later, as a member of the 101st Airborne Division, he would have to go. He wanted to put it behind him. "There was a war, and he felt he was needed and he chose to defend his country."

Shortly before leaving for Vietnam, he married his high school girlfriend, Carol, whom Jimmy called Duck, and by the time he went off to war he knew he was going to be a father. One of the last things he said to his buddy in Vietnam was "I hope my wife has a boy and he loves her as much as I do."

According to his buddy, Jimmy inspired the men around him. He told Mrs. Barbour, "Jimmy was a brave person and Jimmy was not afraid to die. He was an encouragement to all of us. Many times we felt like giving up and he kept encouraging us to carry on."

The chopper pilot who took Jimmy to the hospital in Saigon said that when he picked him up in the field he heard so many people saying "Get Barbour, get Barbour" that he thought he must be an officer. He wiped the blood off Jimmy's nameplate to make sure that he had the right man. He said Jimmy was shot when he put down his rifle in order to help pull out wounded friends.

Evelyn Barbour was out to dinner with Jimmy's pregnant wife, Carol, when the Army came to tell the family that he was dead. She remembers pulling up to the house and seeing cars all around. Both families were there, and the minister from their church had arrived. When Evelyn saw her husband come out the front door with an Army officer behind him, she ran off. "I ran through the woods. I don't know who got me. I blanked out."

When Jimmy's body came home from Vietnam, she was not allowed to kiss him good-bye, something that upsets her to this day. But she was able to see him through the glass cover of the coffin. "I really didn't see how I could let him go. I know I haven't let him go. I nearly died that night of his funeral."

What steadied her in those first awful months was the love of her husband and their son, Wayne, and the birth of Jimmy's baby, James C. Barbour III. Little Jimmy has done a lot of his growing up in and around his grandparents' house. Thursday night is still boys' night out, and he and his grandfather do something together. When he spends the night at his grandparents' house, he sleeps in his dad's bedroom, which is still decorated the way it was when his father was alive.

Evelyn feels closer to her son in the cemetery than in front of the granite panels in Washington. Sometimes, in the summer, she will take a picnic lunch and sit by his grave; she says this "helps as much as anything."

The memorial in Washington has a different feeling for her. Mostly, Evelyn says, it makes her feel numb. "I think the monument is a beautiful thing. It is just so hard to stand there and look at his name and believe he died. It is just so hard to believe. . . . Here is a boy who walked out the door, and ten months and three days later, he's dead. Here's his name on a wall, a hero. It's just hard to connect these things, they happened so fast.

"Everybody that knew us said we was the closest four they had ever seen, and all of a sudden, in a matter of months, it's just all taken from you. You just wonder why something like this had to happen when everybody was so happy."

*Even though I never really knew you, you still meant the world to
me. Thank you, Daddy, for giving me three years of your life.
Remembering you through photos, I can only say I love you, Daddy.
Happy Father's Day. Part of me died with you.*

Love,
Your son
Joe

May 1986

To: Ted Misheikis, Jr.

I'm standing at the Vietnam Memorial today as I've done several times before; the same feeling comes over me—that day in March 1966 was a tough one. I don't know how I survived—by all rights, my wounds should have killed me too. It wasn't easy seeing you laying in that rice paddy. It took me five years to see your folks, but I was glad that I did. I don't know if I'll ever be back here again. In case I don't, let me say, "So Long buddy." I know God is taking care of you. Friends always,

Lee Banicki

C Co., 1st Battalion, 18th Infantry

MICHAEL "BAT" MASTERSON

Lieutenant Colonel, U.S. Air Force, 602nd Special
Operations Squadron
MAY 16, 1937–OCTOBER 13, 1968
Missing in Action

To: Michael "Bat" Masterson

Well here you are, making another lasting impression on me and everyone else who sees you! I love you so much. I have dreamed of the day you'll come home and finally be my Dad. You would have been the best Daddy in the whole world. You were for the short period of time in my life. I can never forget you. I'm 23 now! I sure look a lot different from six years old. You'd be very proud of me. They say I'm a lot like you. I can see it too. I have never forgotten you. I knew you were Santa Claus, but I didn't want to spoil it for you.

Your daughter,
Sheri

———•———

IT WAS their first and their last Christmas together as a family. Cookies and milk were left for Santa Claus and the girls were allowed to sleep with their mother and stepfather in their big round fur-trimmed bed. Sheri, who was five, remembers stirring in her sleep. Her new dad was wide awake. "Can you hear the reindeer? Listen! Can you hear the reindeer?"

"I think he was more excited than the kids," his wife, Fran, remembers. In fact, he was the one to awaken the children on Christmas morning. They were not allowed to open the shutter doors between the bedroom and the living room until he had the camera ready and gave the signal.

Michael "Bat" Masterson had abandoned his bachelorhood a month earlier when he married Fran Randle on Eglin Air Force Base in Fort Walton, Florida. The two had dated for several years, and her two daughters, Sheri and Sue, already seemed like his own. Christmas, 1967, was when it all came together and they were finally a family. Ten months later, on a night mission over Laos, Bat's plane crashed and he became an MIA.

In his last radio transmission he said, "I have vertigo and I'm bailing out." The gyroscope had failed on the small AIG "Sandy" plane Bat was piloting, and without that instrument, it is difficult to know if your plane is flying right side up. The pilot in the plane behind him thought he saw Bat bail out; about forty seconds later he saw the fiery flames as the plane crashed.

Bat Masterson was thirty-one years old at the time. Today he may be dead, or he may have just turned fifty. No one really knows.

He was the only person Sheri ever called Dad, and her memories of him are vivid "because there were never any new ones to take their place." He smelled like English Leather and got a kick out of being silly. "I remember him always pulling a coin out of my ear and I wondered, How can he do it? I thought I just had dimes coming in and out of my ears!"

The two of them pulled off a fine caper one afternoon. Her mother was ironing, chatting with Bat, and watching *The Dating Game*, and Sheri was supposed to be taking a nap; but she wanted to be in the dining room, where the fun was, and she made repeated appearances. Finally her mother warned her that if she came in once more, she'd be spanked.

Discipline was not one of Bat's strong suits. When Sheri appeared again, he was supposed to take her back into her room for punishment. He closed the bedroom door and began to plead, "Sheri, you have to take a nap and if you promise to take a nap I won't give you a spanking, but your mom thinks I'm going to spank you so . . . " Bat began clapping his hands loudly and Sheri began to cry on cue. It was years before her mother knew what had happened.

"He was one of the happy people," his wife recalls. He loved to make people laugh. Nothing was sacred. Toward the end of their wedding ceremony, as she and Bat knelt together at the front of the chapel, she became aware that the congregation was trying to suppress chuckles and chortles. Bat had printed, in bold letters, H-E on his left shoe and L-P on his right shoe. That was Bat.

"He couldn't understand people that were depressed. He would come bouncing into the house and if somebody was in a bad mood, he'd sit down and ask you why you didn't have a good day."

Born in Canada, Bat grew up in Washington State, and majored in engineering in college. "He was a warrior who didn't like war," Fran says; she thinks he would have liked to perform with the Thunderbirds at some point. In Laos he flew rescue missions for the most part, and preferred them to bombing runs.

Sheri was six when Bat was shot down. It was hard for her to grasp what had happened. "I thought, Missing? How could he be missing? Doesn't he know where he is? Then I thought, If he is missing, they'll find him."

She remembers fantasizing that if only she had tripped her father before he left for Vietnam, he might have broken a leg and been able to stay home. After school, she'd sit on the front steps, waiting for the mailman. The Mastersons knew a family whose first word of their MIA came four years after he was shot down, when the mailman brought them a letter the man had sent from Hanoi. There was always a reason to hope.

Fran's search for her husband began immediately after the Air Force officers arrived at her home in their shiny blue car to tell her of Bat's disappearance. Her quest has been relentless. She took her two daughters with her on trips to Thailand, Hong Kong, Laos, and back and forth across the United States, looking for clues, leads, facts, any bit of information she could unearth. She has been to every meeting of the National League of Families for the past eighteen years and has picketed the White House and the Chinese embassy. "I remember telling the girls, 'Smile. He might be in China.' "

Today Fran and her daughters are tired and they are angry at the way the U.S. government has handled the POW/MIA issue. But they are not about to give up. "We keep saying, next year, we won't have to do this. But in the back of our minds, we know we have been saying this for years. If someone told me I'd have to keep going for another ten years, I'd probably quit right now, thinking I can't do that. But I've done it. And you just keep doing it, one day at a time," Sheri says.

Both women feel Hanoi held on to prisoners of war as bargaining chips. They think that Nixon and Kissinger had every intention of bringing them home, but that that intent was thwarted when Congress imposed a bombing halt and when Watergate discredited the administration. It became easier to write off the POWs and presume them dead than to deal with the North Vietnamese, who were demanding the three billion dollars in war reparations they had been promised. POW/MIA activists like the Mastersons believe successive administrations added layer upon layer to the cover-up rather than face the staggering embarrassment and blame that would follow if the truth were known.

"Bureaucrats lie and evade to protect themselves, and then they try to make it seem as though the families can't face reality," Fran says. She mentions one argument that was used to blunt the outspokenness of POW/MIA families: "You've got to be quiet or nobody will ever go into the military again."

Like many others, Fran didn't really question the war in the early sixties, but after Bat disappeared in Laos, she started to read history. "I read about the French war and how they hadn't released all the French prisoners at the end and how they were torturing them." She expresses her feelings about the Vietnam War in three words: "It was crazy." Is she bitter? "You better believe I am bitter about the war. And what scares me is that they're trying to get another one going in Central America. It scares me."

Sheri adds, "It's hard to say that all those people were killed for nothing, but that's how it seems. It hurt more people than it helped."

Sheri still dreams about her dad. "About a week ago, I dreamed that he was here. He had been home for a while, everything was normal. He was still young. I came over and my car wasn't working and I asked him to fix it for me. . . . I was very nonchalant. In my dream I kept staring at him."

In one of her bad dreams, Sheri is strapped to a plane seat in a desert. She sees a plane come in and she knows that it's Bat's. It crashes into the ground. "I'm screaming, 'Bat, get out!' and the plane is cut in half and he's right there. One half of him is a skeleton and one half is totally normal and he just looks at me in total desperation."

She continues to hope. When the phone rings at an odd hour, her first thought is that it's Norton Air Force Base saying, "Come on, your dad's out here, come pick him up." But she knows that if he does come home, the reality could be harsh. "Will he remember us? Will he be in the hospital a long time? Our whole lives are going to be totally changed. My life will revolve totally around him."

And then, like the amiable and pretty Southern Californian she is, Sheri's happy thoughts take over. "I can see me going, 'Remember how you liked Corvettes? Well, these are the new models and these are calculators and look at these video games.' I'd go out and buy him everything, just to show him stuff."

Sheri Masterson's trip to the Vietnam Veterans Memorial in July 1985 was unexpectedly satisfying. She went with a friend whose dad is also missing, and because of a series of meetings and commitments that lasted into the night, they didn't get to the memorial until two-thirty in the morning. "The sky was orange. We walked down there. I didn't realize that there were that many men. The first thing you do is go across his name with your finger, very slowly. It was really hot that night and I started crying.''

She walked the length of the memorial and read some of the messages and notes that had been left. One said, ''She looks just like you.''

Even though it was close to dawn, people were still at the memorial. Sheri felt safe and protected. ''There is an energy there that is unreal. . . . I knew he knew that I was trying to reach out and let him know that I'm okay. He knows that I'm worried about him. . . . I wanted him not to worry about me. I wanted him to know that I'm okay, that I turned out very good and that he should be proud of me and how well Mom did.

''I really didn't think anyone was going to read my letter. I got out a pencil and just wrote. I felt a lot better. I can't express the feeling I had after writing it. I wrote as much as I could. . . . When I set it down and I stood up and I wiped my tears, I knew, either alive or dead, he knew that I had just made contact with him.''

Dearest Chuck,

This is the first time I've written you since April, 1970. But I know you wouldn't think it silly. I've written a lot of poems from my heartache of being without you. I wish that you weren't shipped out on that early flight. We would have been married before you left. Not seeing you after made it hard for me to believe. I looked for you in the face of every young man. I thought about having your baby and making love to you. We really were ripped off of the most beautiful things in life.

They told me you didn't die right away. God I hope you didn't suffer too badly. It's not fair. They didn't know how gentle you were, how precious. I wonder if I'll see you in heaven. I dream occasionally. They say you then know of my love. Remember the letter you wrote? When you said you were fighting a war you didn't understand? It seemed no one really understood. We were only 19 then babe and here I am, 16 years later, still wondering. I went to the cemetery once in California where they buried you. I hope you saw me. This is all very hard for me. Even now I still have the ring you gave me and all the poems and pictures. I have a special friend now who understands all of this. He listens to the story of how we met and all the crazy things we did. He knows how much I love you even now. It's the only thing that did not die or end. God be with you Chuck. I'll always dream of you.

Love,
Cher

Dear David,

Just thought I'd write, when I wrote this letter, I'd never seen a clearer night. The breeze was blowing gently like the ones you always enjoyed, and the crickets still can sing me off to sleep.

Talked to Kate the other day on the telephone. She said she's doing better, trying to adjust to being alone. She said she's going to take some classes in the fall, you said you'd take one with her when you got home, as you recall.

Well, Mom's been meaning to see you, but the work's just never done, and Dad just seems to sit around and stare. Well, I just know they're real proud of you. You served your country like you had to do. It'll take a little time, but they'll be there.

I guess I miss you most of all. You were more than a brother, you were my friend. I thought we'd be together, but so suddenly it had to end, I never thought I'd never see you again. I would have stood out by the airport, waiting for your flight to be called, I didn't think we'd see your name up on that wall.

Hell Train

Traveling off to Boot Camp, enlisted in the Corps.
The Hell of San Diego to be followed by much more.
Guaranteed no rose garden, just built into a man.
Ordered only to serve and survive the very best I can.
The eagle, globe, and anchor, the emblem of the Corps.
Worn on the cover of the uniform that I so proudly wore.
It meant "Marine" to others, it was there so they could tell.
It also meant I'd earned a one-way ticket straight to Hell.
I volunteered for combat duty, I must have been insane.
I wanted to join that group of men who rode that Hell-bound train.
Many men had gone before me, and some did not return.
I thought I'd go and find some glory, but I was soon to learn.
There is no glory in Viet Nam, just hate and death and pain.
It hit me hard and cut me deep when I stepped off that train.
Nam was worse than anything I had ever seen or heard.
Twelve long months would pass before I saw the Freedom Bird.
Viet Nam has certain smells that cannot be forgotten.
Blood and gunpowder, sweat and smoke, dead things that are rotten.
The sights I saw, the things I did, the sounds I came to know,
Stay with me now and grab my mind with hands that won't let go.
I returned to the world I left before, but things were out of place.
People treated me like scum, and spit insults in my face.
All their ignorant abuse confused me, my mind became quite hazy.
Soon the protected and ungrateful people convinced me I was crazy.
I lived alone in my crazy world, convinced my mind had fled.
Nights became the worst of all, my days were filled with dread.
Something was gnawing at my mind, and ticking like a bomb.
I slowly realized that I was still in Viet Nam.
Nam was locked up in my head, and I couldn't get it out.
It drove me mad, it froze my heart, it made me rage and shout.
I turned into another man, just who I didn't know.
That bomb was getting awful hot, and just about to blow.
I had to find out who I was, and just who I was not.
I hadn't run to Canada to keep from getting shot.
I didn't hide in college, or toss my draft card in a flame.

I wasn't a homosexual, and I wasn't blind or lame.
I wasn't hooked on dope or booze, I'd never robbed a store.
I'd never raped or killed someone, I'd never had a whore.
I was just an American teenaged boy with a heavy obligation.
Being an able-bodied male, I had to serve the nation.
Given this thankless duty to do, I did it and did it well.
But there was no welcome home for me when I came back from Hell.
No gratitude or appreciation from the ones who never helped out.
I just found out the hard way what life is all about.
Now I know just who I am, the facts are plain to see.
There's a price in life for everything, and nothing comes for free.
I paid my dues, I earned my stripes, I have the right to live.
Forever bitter, I won't forget, and I never will forgive.
I'll never be taken in again, and used up till I'm gone.
I'll do what's best for me and mine, and just keep pushing on.
If the protected can't recognize these facts, at least I know I can.
It doesn't matter what others think, I'm proud and I'm a man.

Michael "MAD MIKE" Sargent
VIETNAM COMBAT VETERAN
Corporal 2697813 U.S.M.C.

GEARWIN PHILLIP TOUSEY

Private First Class, Company C, 5th Battalion, 60th Infantry,
9th Infantry Division
OCTOBER 12, 1944–FEBRUARY 25, 1968

In Memory of Gearwin P. Tousey

Sometime as I sit in the sun
My mind wanders back to days gone by
I see a small boy, all goldenly brown
He wears polos, bib overalls and runs barefoot on the ground
But mostly, he wears a gleam in his eye.
He climbs trees, rides bikes, plays in mud puddles
Steps on ants and throws stones high across the sky
He's five, his days are busy playing in the sun.

I see a boy half grown, all goldenly brown
He wears a white wool uniform, tennies and a cap pulled down
Across his shoulders is marked "CHAMPS"
But mostly, he wears a gleam in his eye
He rides a two-wheel bike with a catcher's mitt hung on the bar
He can bat a ball way, way out and come in home, safe on a fly
He's ten, his days are busy playing in the sun.

I see a youth not really a boy, not really a man, all goldenly brown
He wears white polos, blue jeans, tennies
And a one-sided grin that implies "I'm shy."
But mostly, he wears a gleam in his eye.
He's a star football halfback on cold afternoons
But when cold afternoons turn into spring
You can hear crowds sing "GO TOUS GO" and with flying wings
He jumps the last hurdle and dashes for the string.
He works part-time too after school to buy some wheels soon
He's fifteen, his days are busy playing in the sun.

I see a young man, all grown and golden brown.
He wears hip-huggers, starched ironed shirts,
Shining new loafers and shades
But mostly, he wears a gleam in his eye.
His school days are behind him but his friends all have stayed.
He works every day now, makes plans for his future days
He likes a night out to laugh and joke and shoot pool with the guys
He's twenty, and his days are numbered to play in the sun.

I see a good-looking man, all goldenly brown
He wears an Army uniform now with medals and bars and braid

But mostly, he wears a gleam in his eye.
He's a soldier now, his country has called
Because he's grown straight and tall in both body and mind.
He must go to fight in the jungles of a far-off land
But here, soft in our hand, he leaves his heart
This golden-golden man
He's twenty-three and off to war
And his days in the sun will be no more.

———————•———————

ON MARCH 13, 1986, eighteen years to the day after his memorial service, Gary Tousey's mother and sister touched his name on Panel 41 East, Line 27, of the Vietnam Veterans Memorial.

Neither Georgia Tousey nor Donna Ferron had ever flown on an airplane before they flew from Green Bay, Wisconsin, to Washington, D.C., to run their fingertips across the twenty letters grit-blasted into the granite. They had spent all morning looking for an artificial wreath to bring for him. It was still too wintry for fresh flowers, and they wanted something that would last until Easter. His sister Donna pinned to the wreath a poem she had written the year after he died. His mother wept. "It bothered me. I had to break down and have my tears. In my mind, he was home in Green Bay, lying in the cemetery. But it was an honor to see his name."

Donna did not cry, but she found the experience overwhelming. "Seeing all those names—and they are all gone—and all those names touch to other people and how many millions of people must be involved. I'm glad there is some recognition that these boys gave their lives for our country. That I am happy for. I hope it is healing for others.

"We always called him the sunshine of our life—people that got to know him wherever we lived nicknamed him Sunshine. He always had that big smile." He was an extroverted child and brought a world of delightful commotion into the Tousey family. His sisters were fifteen and ten when he was born. Donna remembers him "small and mischievous, riding his tricycle around the dining room, poking his lead pencil into my arm—he was just a boy."

Gary's favorite subject in school was math, and football was his favorite sport. He excelled as an athlete and wanted to go to college and be a football star, but when the time came, he had the ability but not the money. So he started to work and was training to be an engineer on the Milwaukee railroad when his draft notice came.

It would have been easy for him to have a deferment because he was a father. He had a son from a brief marriage that ended in divorce and a daughter from his second marriage, which was satisfying and secure. He adored his children, and yet he felt compelled to go into the Army, even though he knew it would probably mean Vietnam.

It was a tradition on his father's side of the family; he and five of his brothers served in World War II. The Touseys are American Indians; family legend has it that their ancestors participated in the sale of Manhattan. The family had migrated west and become part of the Sockbridge/Muncie tribe. Gary's mother is part Muncie as well. Although they never lived on a reservation or were active in Native American issues, they are proud of their heritage and proud of their patriotism.

"Gary went for his country, his family, for us. He would rather go and fight communism over there than have it come here, to us, his family," his sister recalls. "Gary went with the view that he was going for us. He signed all his letters, 'Your protector, Gary.' "

He loved the camaraderie of the Army, and if he had any doubts about going to Vietnam, he kept them to himself. When he left in a snowstorm for the jungles of Southeast Asia, his plane was delayed for hours, and the family was on edge, waiting for his departure. "No tears, no tears, remember, no tears," was what he kept saying. Their last image of him was his waving good-bye with a newspaper from an airplane window as small as a postage stamp. In one of his first letters home, he told them that saying good-bye to his family was one of the hardest things he had ever had to do.

He was stationed with the Ninth Infantry Division in the Mekong Delta. He had been in Vietnam for only six weeks when his family had a first inkling of trouble. "We tuned in the radio to get the correct time, and a news broadcast reported that in the early hours the Ninth Infantry Division had a sneak attack at their base camp. With a prayer on our lips, we left for church."

The next evening, an Army sergeant came and told Mary Tousey, Gary's wife, that her husband was missing. The following morning, the same sergeant returned to tell her that Gary was dead, killed with nineteen others in a Viet Cong attack on February 25, 1968.

His mother wrote in her diary:

*How can I tell you how much like death life was at that instant? I
pictured you as clearly as ever I have seen you, in all the ways I've ever
seen; as a chubby baby drooling on my shoulder, as a Little Leaguer
straining as a catcher to throw down to second base, as a fiery captain
of your hockey team, as a rugged halfback giving his all for the West
High Wildcats, "Go Tous Go!" the games you so dearly loved as you
asked, "Mom, do you think there will be football in heaven?" I saw
you grown—a man blooming in pride in the Army uniform, so strong
and tough and openly sentimental. And I thought of you, Gary, shot
down in battle. Certainly a mistake. That you could die was unthink-
able.*

When his body came home sixteen days later, the family had the
sealed casket opened to make sure there was no mistake. Donna's
husband, Marvin, confirmed that it was Gary.

Before Gary left for Vietnam, he had given his wife a ten-dollar bill
and asked her to buy his mother red roses for Mother's Day. He had
never done anything like that before. When they were delivered to
Georgia Tousey a few months after he died, she was stunned. "I
came in the front door and there was this great big bouquet of roses
on one of the chairs. I looked at the card and it said, 'From your son.'
That pretty near killed me."

Donna and her family still live in the Green Bay area; she helps with
the books for her husband's filling station. Their four sons and two
daughters range in age from twenty-eight to twelve. She had never
written poetry before her brother died and had no special interest in
it. The poems just arose, like vapor from the earth, in the year following his death. She wrote four, one of which she left at the Vietnam
Veterans Memorial.

"I would just write. Something would come into my head when I
was ironing, and I would just write. Just for a year. And I couldn't
put two words together right now if I had to. I didn't know how to
construct a poem, I didn't follow any form. I think that poem that
you read was written in an afternoon's time. It was easy to write
because it was Gary."

She had one morbid dream about her brother in the year after he died: she was searching for him among row after row of soldiers' bodies laid out on cots. Once, her husband, Marvin, who generally ridicules such things, felt Gary's presence so strongly in the basement that he threw down his hammer and came upstairs. The Easter after Gary died, Marvin saw him appear in the hallway in his uniform, salute, turn, and walk away. After that the visions ceased.

As 1986 came to a close, a totally unexpected event brought Gary back into his family's life. A young college student named Amy Berger had asked the court to open her adoption records, a necessary procedure if she was to get the education benefits she was entitled to as a Native American. Amy was a child of Gary and his wife, Mary, born before their marriage and given up for adoption. When she learned who her birth parents were, and that her father had died in Vietnam, she wrote to Mary, who sent her back a long letter about Gary.

Amy said, "As I read her letter I began to cry. I felt sorrow because of his death. It's not the same kind of sorrow you feel when you lose someone you know. I'm sorry for what happened to him, but also because I lost the hope of ever knowing him. . . . It's an empty, sad feeling to know that I will never see the smile that Grandma Tousey says I have, or be able to hug the man who created me and tell him that, in my heart, I have always loved him.

"I would say part of me feels cheated. Not only for myself, but for his other children, and for our father, too. It's not fair that he had to die at such a young age and miss out on his family and watching his children grow. It's not right that he could not be here to share in the reunion of me and my birth family."

The family was reunited with Amy at Christmas. Her mother and sister flew in from California, and her brother joined them too, with the other relatives, at Grandma Tousey's house. They played Amy a tape that her father had sent home from Vietnam. "When I heard the tape of his voice," Amy says, "I had to hold back the tears. All I could think of was that he never once saw me, and there I was hearing his voice. To hear him tell my mother how much he loved her and that he would be careful was heart-wrenching."

Grandma Tousey gave Amy her father's Purple Heart, because she wanted her newest granddaughter "to always be proud of her dad and his supreme sacrifice." She also shared with Amy the pages from her journal in which she tried to say good-bye to Gary.

How, my son, do I say farewell?

The red roses you ordered for Mother's Day, 1968, for me, were just beautiful. It was as if in all finality, you were thanking me and telling me of the love we shared together. The red paint on the big tree where you sprayed your hot rod engine is fading away. Dad will always cherish the railroad watch you left in his car. Your tools are just as you left them in the garage.

We wear our gold stars for you and are proud of your medals; our son, who fell in another world than ours, desiring freedom for others, dedicating his own freedom to what he believed was noble. We are keeping fresh the good memories and more often now, as we speak of you, it is with joy.

We who loved you and buried you thank you eternally. America has had no better than you, and you were ours.

Your Mom

Goodbye, Gary, Goodbye

My Friend—

   I came today to find your name. To remember.

   I remember training. The dirt and the sweat. I remember laughing, the drink and the girls. I remember you. The confidence and strength. We were invincible then.

   The world has changed. I am sorry you don't share it with me. I am sorry your name is here. I ask why mine is not.

   One slain, one spared. I cannot answer. It is too much for me. We had never thought of it before. Remember? The dirt and the sweat, the drink and the girls.

   I leave you now. Rest in peace, my fallen friend. One small measure for your great sacrifice: I leave a tear at your wall. And I will carry your memory forever.

   I came today to find your name. To remember.

EDWARD VAN EVERY, JR.

Specialist Five, 335th Radio Research Company,
Delta Military Assistance Command
DECEMBER 8, 1947–JUNE 1, 1970

June 8, 1985

Dear Eddie,

    Although it's been fifteen years since you've been gone, it feels like it could have been fifteen days. Many times I have regretted not getting to know you better than I did. There was a quiet, sensitive goodness about you. You were one of the guys that had been with the unit awhile and was getting "short." I knew about your girl, your Mom & Dad and that you wanted to put your time in and get home. If anyone knew you at all, they liked you a lot.

    I'll never forget being awakened at three that morning by the hysterical crying of Denny Newbill and Jerry Hall. "One of our guys is—!" was all I could get out of Newbill. When Jerry told me it was you, I can remember demanding an answer—"Oh God, Why? Why any of us? Why Eddie?" I never did get any concrete answers. Our whole company felt a tremendous loss. When I left in August, there was still a sense of grief around. Things never did get back to "normal."

    I hope you don't mind, but recently I made contact with your parents. They've moved twice and are now retired in Missouri, trusting in the Lord that you are at peace. They can't afford to travel much, so I've sent them pictures of the Memorial and your name. They're good people, too. I hope to meet them some day.

    For years, I felt your life, as well as the other 58,000 lives, was wasted, and anyone who wasn't there could not or would not understand what we went through. That's changing now. People are beginning to realize that we were doing our jobs and doing them well. We had to pay the price and until recently, we were the ones tagged as losers, not our government. So if your names on this wall make it harder to send guys half way round the world to die, then maybe it wasn't a total waste.

    I love you, brother. I pray some day we can welcome each other home. Peace.

                              John "Soup" Campbell
                              335th Radio Research Co.

                              Can Tho, Vietnam
                              August 1969 to August 1970

LIKE Eddie Van Every, John Campbell had a desk job in Vietnam. He never picked a leech from his skin or slept in cold mud. Yet the war came home with him as surely as it did with any grunt.

When you meet him today, his openness and geniality seem utterly spontaneous. But John "Soup" Campbell came home from Vietnam with a devastating secret in his heart and for years told no one about it.

He had killed a man, a sniper who was crouched in a tree, preparing to fire at John and five of his friends. John just happened to see a small rustle in the leaves. He said, "I saw something," and someone said, "Shoot," and he did.

He became an unwilling hero of the 335th Radio Research Company, stationed in the Mekong Delta near Can Tho. His commanding officer wanted to put him in for a Bronze Star. His buddies were envious; their unit saw virtually no combat. John said he did not want the medal and would not accept it. Although it may be unrelated to the incident, the Army promoted him a rank several weeks later.

Three months later he left Vietnam and resumed his quiet and secure life. His wife, Betsy, was thrilled to have him back; his parents fussed over him. For the next fourteen years, whenever the family mentioned John's tour in Vietnam, they added, "But at least he didn't have to kill anyone."

John grew up in Woodbury, New Jersey. His family lived next door to the Methodist church they attended, and John went to Sunday school, belonged to the youth group, and participated in the Wednesday-night prayer meetings. He believed that killing was wrong. He understood that it happened but he was determined never to be a part of it.

The Army recruiter assured him, practically guaranteed him, that he would never have to go to Vietnam if he enlisted and asked for data processing. The Army didn't even have computer equipment in Vietnam of the kind he'd be trained for. It seemed a safe bet, but by his twenty-first birthday he had his orders for Nam.

His tour went well, however—until the moment he saw that movement in the leaves. In an instant his life was changed.

"When I came back, I told myself I had the whole thing licked. It wasn't a big deal. There were plenty of guys over there who had gone through a whole lot more than I did, and they did it day after day. But it just blew my mind how anybody could hold their act together after having gone through something like that, when I just had a little taste of it and I knew what it did to me."

He was angry at God and he felt betrayed. He had tried to be a good person. He had played by the rules. Why had he been the one to pull that trigger?

He did his best to put his Vietnam experience behind him, and he never talked about being a vet. That began to change in 1982, when he and his wife went to the dedication of the Vietnam Veterans Memorial. He wore his uniform and marched in the parade with the contingent from New Jersey. For the first time, it didn't seem like such a bad thing to be a vet; some guys seemed almost to rejoice in it. Strangers were hugging him and saying "Welcome home."

At the memorial he looked for the name of the one man in his unit who had died in Vietnam. It wasn't there. Campbell was convinced a mistake had been made, and he was determined to set it right. He was going to find the man's family and tell them that his name was not on the memorial.

But he had the wrong name. In the twelve years since he had been in Vietnam, his memory had blurred the name Van Every into Van Lear. Eventually, however, he found someone in the casualty records section of the Pentagon who was willing to help him. Campbell supplied dates and detailed unit information, and his contact called back and said, "I've found your man."

The name of Edward Van Every, Jr., is on the memorial, but Campbell wanted to talk to his family anyway, and to find out more about him. After a dozen or more phone calls he finally located the Van Everys; they had moved twice since Eddie's death, but a postmaster was able to help Campbell track them down. The Van Everys were touched. No one from their son's unit had ever tried to reach them. A correspondence began, and John sent them pictures of the memorial, which they had never visited.

Eddie Van Every—everyone called him Junior—grew up in a white frame farmhouse in Hampton, Iowa. There were ice-cream socials at the church in summer and sledding in winter. The family raised corn, alfalfa, chickens, and pigs, and life was as predictable as the turn of the seasons. Farming was a family affair then. "You're just one big unit," Eddie's father said. "We all worked together and played together. That's what I call living. A lot of hard work, but a lot of fun."

Eddie was a gentle, quiet person, according to those who knew him. He was a long-distance runner and played first trombone in the high school band. After a year in junior college he enlisted in the Army instead of waiting to be drafted. The Army trained him as a linguist, and after an assignment in Germany, he was sent to Vietnam. He worked in radio intelligence, monitoring and interpreting enemy communications. It was important work but not dangerous. Eddie's death was an accident, the result of a fall.

After getting in touch with the Van Everys, John Campbell felt he had at last accomplished something positive in connection with Vietnam. The healing process that had begun with his trip to the dedication of the memorial in 1982 was strengthened by his successful effort to reach the family of a man he hardly knew. But it was not yet complete.

He realized that he was becoming increasingly aggressive. His temper was easily triggered, and although he never struck out at his family, he saw that his anger could drive him that far. He was scared enough to seek help.

He went to see a counselor and confessed his secret. The therapist explained to him that his Vietnam experience could be the source of his aggressive feelings and advised him to tell his story to the people who mattered to him. That night John Campbell went to his parents' home and told them that fourteen years ago he had killed a man in Vietnam. Later in the evening he told his wife.

They were shocked—not by what he had done but by the knowledge that he had kept it hidden from them for years. He seemed to have come home from Vietnam unscarred. He had a happy marriage, two children, Martin and Michele, whom he adored, secure roots in his church and his community. Yet for years he had been carrying a burden they would gladly have helped him to bear.

It was not until he was able to share his secret with his family that John Campbell finally came to terms with his Vietnam experience. When he left his letter to Eddie Van Every at the memorial in 1985, he did so, he says, to tell people about Eddie and to tell the country —and himself—that he was proud to be a Vietnam veteran.

Daddy,

Came by again to see your name, funny how that's all I have. Today's my birthday. I really do miss you and wish you'll come home soon. Maybe they will release you tomorrow. Please, Daddy, remember me. I think of you always and miss you terribly. I love you, we all do. Please be safe. 'Til Later!

I love you,
Your baby girl always
Peanuts

DAN LEE NEELY

Private First Class, Bravo Company, 2nd Battalion,
7th Cavalry Regiment, 1st Cavalry Division (Airmobile)
APRIL 27, 1948–MARCH 1, 1968

RODOLFO VALENZUELA

Private First Class, Bravo Company, 2nd Battalion,
7th Cavalry Regiment, 1st Cavalry Division (Airmobile)
SEPTEMBER 4, 1947–MARCH 1, 1968

Dear Dan and Rudy,

    I was your leader and I have not forgotten you. Nor have I forgotten how you each gave your lives to rescue wounded comrades from a nameless hill in a worthless country. I'm sorry I never wrote your families back then, but I was wounded myself a few days later and I lost touch with everyone in the hospital. I have finally begun to write my, and our, story after eighteen years. I haven't gotten to March 1, 1968, yet. I had to come down last night and tell you about it before I wrote about it. I also wanted to spend a little time alone with you on the night before you die again. I wanted to be with you again when the clock struck midnight and your numbers came up. It felt good and I appreciate your talking to me.

    Attached is my diary entry for that terrible day. I'm sorry I couldn't write more then, but I was too full of sadness, rage and bitterness over losing you. And of course you know we had another mission the next day. There wasn't much time for goodbyes, but "C'est la guerre." In the last few years, I have begun to find more inner peace, thanks to a lot of good brothers and sisters who served with us.

    It is important for people to know how and why you died. And it is important for your families to know that you did not die alone, or in vain. Your friends were with you to the bitter end.

    I am trying to locate your families now, so I can offer to share with them my memories of you. I hope their bitterness has eased enough for them to want to hear the story of your death.

            Love always,
            Daniel Grattan Doyle, Jr.
            1st Lieutenant, Infantry
            3rd Platoon, Bravo Company,
            2nd Battalion
            7th Cavalry Regiment, 1st Cavalry
            Division (Airmobile)

THIS WAS not a big battle with a memorable name but a stupid little skirmish on a scruffy hump of a hill. They couldn't even see the enemy, entrenched in a camouflaged bunker. Within a few hours two men were killed and eleven were wounded. It was the sort of thing that happened day after day, year after year, in Vietnam. The date was March 1, 1968.

First Lieutenant Dan Doyle's platoon of thirty men was sent out to reinforce another platoon that had come under sniper fire. Army intelligence had concluded that there was a North Vietnamese regimental headquarters in the area between Hue and the DMZ. Dan's platoon was part of a battalion that was in the region to ferret it out.

As the platoon moved out, a man was wounded. Two others went forward to rescue him, and they were wounded too. The three men had apparently fallen within thirty feet of an enemy bunker. Each time a rescue attempt was made, more men were wounded.

Dan could see that the morale of his men was eroding. He decided that since he was their leader, he would lead a rescue attempt himself. His men laid down the covering fire, and he crawled out and pulled Smitty to safety.

That left two wounded men still out there. He asked for volunteers to help rescue them, and Dan Neely, his radioman, volunteered. As he inched forward, he lifted up to fire and was shot in the head. The twenty-year-old from Alabama, whose nickname was Preacher Boy, was dead.

Rudy Valenzuela was the machine gunner who was spewing out covering fire from behind a bush. He never saw the grenade that landed in front of the barrel of his gun.

Dan Doyle got to him first and held him in his arms, cradling his head in his lap. "Don't let me die. I want to go home." Home was in Gilbert, Arizona. He had never been away from it before.

"I knew he wasn't going to live as soon as he put his head in my lap. There was nothing I could do to save his life," Dan says. "Rudy was really dying then, and the only thing I could have given him, I gave him. He didn't die alone. That was the most important thing; it was the only thing that mattered."

Eventually, gunships and medevac choppers came in and canisters of white phosphorus were fired to provide a shroud of smoke so that the wounded could be retrieved. Dan watched Rudy being put on a medevac chopper and broke down. He had forgotten rule one for an officer: don't get attached to your men. "I remember starting to cry when they took Rudy away and I don't remember seeing anything or hearing anything else. I felt myself teetering on that edge and I remember thinking, This is insanity and if I go over that edge I'm never coming back. Then somebody hugged me. His nickname was Hoss. He was about six feet two and had been drafted out of UCLA, where he was working on his master's degree in English literature. He was the best machine gunner I had. He put his arms around me and hugged me and said, 'It's going to be okay, Three-six, it's going to be okay.' I came out of whatever trance I was in and did what needed to be done."

In his diary he listed the names of the men in his platoon who were dead or wounded and then he wrote: "I got a Silver Star for it. *Big Deal.* It hurts very much, losing so many good, brave men. I hate all these slant-eyed gook bastards. Even the little old ladies and little kids. I grew up that day."

Dan Doyle knows he got off easy. He knows plenty of officers who lost dozens of men and who still hear their screams in the night. For Dan, there are just two: Dan and Rudy. Although there was still plenty of horror and combat to come, that day, March 1, 1968, altered his life irrevocably.

For nineteen years, Levern Neely, Dan Neely's mother, prayed that she would meet someone who would be able to tell her how her boy died. He was born at home, two months prematurely. At birth he weighed two pounds and ten ounces. He was too tiny to nurse, so for the first month of his life, Levern Neely drizzled milk into his mouth with an eyedropper. She never gave up. "I just knew little babies could make it."

Dan Neely was drafted. He didn't want to go. He was a gentle boy who couldn't bear even to hunt. He told his mother, "God gave us these animals to look at, not to kill." His buddies called him Preacher Boy because he never went out into the field without first asking the Lord to take care of him and his friends.

In one of the tapes he sent his mom from Vietnam he told her, "This is Johnson's private war and we got no business being here." In his last letter he said that a lot of guys were getting killed because their M-16 rifles jammed; they needed to be oiled. Levern Neely packed up a box of WD-40 oil to send to Vietnam so her son could fire his rifle properly.

He loved his mama's pinto beans and corn bread with a jug of sweet iced tea to wash it down with. Levern made that for him, along with his other favorite foods, the day he left for Vietnam. She asked him if there was anything else she could do for him before they went to the airport. He said, "Don't go to the airport with me. I want to remember you here in the kitchen. If I don't come back, don't worry, I'll miss you from heaven."

Nineteen years after her son's death, Levern Neely met the person who could tell her the story of how he died. Because his body was missing an arm and a leg when it came home, the family had feared that he died a lingering and painful death. In early 1987, Levern talked to Dan Doyle, who told her he died instantly from a bullet wound to the head; he was maimed after he was killed when a grenade fell nearby. Terrible as it was, this news brought Levern Neely the peace she had prayed for.

Rudy's mother has not been able to speak about her son since the day she learned he had been killed on March 1, 1968. Her nine other children and grandchildren know she won't talk about him, so they don't try. She never talked about Rudy to her husband after his death. A letter arrived from Rudy after he died. His mother read it but did not share it with anyone else.

Rudy was drafted, but he could have had a deferment. His father needed him to help on the Arizona farm he was managing. Rudy thought it was his duty to go to Vietnam. His older sister, Lupe Kramer, says, "He thought Vietnam was going to be a breeze." Rudy loved country-and-western music and liked to be decked out in cowboy hats and boots. His mother had promised him a brand-new pair of boots when he got home from Vietnam, but she bought them before he went. He got to wear them only a few times. His sister says, "It was almost as though my mother thought that if he could wear those boots, he wouldn't have to go to Vietnam."

Dan Doyle, following in his father's footsteps, volunteered to go to Vietnam. Dan was the eldest child and was named after his dad, a career officer in the Army. His father had been kicked out of West Point for failing French, and he had hoped his son would graduate from there. But Dan left college after two years and, just before he was drafted, enlisted in the Army and volunteered for Vietnam. "My father fought in two wars in the infantry. I was going to succeed or not come back. It was my turn to do my duty like my father before me." That attitude changed when Dan and Rudy got killed. "The patriotic part—Save Vietnam for Democracy—that went on March 1. I consider myself a patriot and I would fight for my country, but I would have to think twice about fighting for someone else's country. I came back somewhat a pacifist; at least I have very clear reasons about what I will, and will not, fight for."

After fifteen months in Vietnam, Dan Doyle came home to Charlottesville, Virginia. He was one of the few Vietnam vets whose homecoming offered a sense of belonging rather than ostracism. His dad invited over as many Army buddies of his from Korea and World War II as he could find, and they got out the scotch and a couple of cases of beer and told war stories. Dan was welcomed into the club.

Dan received a Ph.D. in psychology from the University of Tennessee and now runs the vet center in Richmond, Virginia. In a sense, he is doing exactly what he did in Vietnam—guiding men through battle—but this time it's guerrilla warfare with themselves.

"Driving in to work today, I was thinking that I make a distinction between hearts and souls. I was thinking that wounded hearts heal, wounded souls change. This is how I explain the changes in me: I've had broken hearts before, girlfriends, that sort of stuff. I got over it and I was the same. I am not the same person I was before Vietnam."

He thinks the changes he went through on March 1 and during the rest of his tour are typical of what many other vets went through. "We've met our maker at least once, sometimes many times, and lived to walk away from it. That's an experience most people don't have in their lives; they meet their maker once and that's it. So what sets us apart from other people is that we've already been to the end of the road and come back. That mystery isn't there anymore. Actually, I think I died back then and I'm living on borrowed time. I think this life is like a loan or a gift. It's not only free, it's precious, because I didn't expect it."

He has found an equilibrium in his life and he is helping others do the same. He takes his work very seriously. In his desk drawer are a .357 Magnum and a bloodstained knife, relinquished by two of his deeply disturbed clients. Most of the men he works with are decent, hardworking guys who are trying to make a go of their lives and to extricate themselves from a web of combat traumas, a condition that is often diagnosed as PTSD, post-traumatic stress disorder.

Because Richmond is only ninety miles from Washington, D.C., the Vietnam Veterans Memorial has been an integral part of Dan's professional work and of his personal healing. He has been there about twenty times.

"I don't hear any voices, but those pieces of my heart come back, some of those empty spaces fill up, those holes in my head or holes in my soul feel full. I am not alone. I feel like I am in company. That's where I go to find my men and the pieces of me that are still tied to them.

"You need to go to the wall the first time with someone you trust —or in a group as often as you like. But the end point of therapy is to be able to go alone and stay a significant amount of time by yourself. Facing it alone is kind of a last test."

Dan is in the process of writing a book about his own experience in Vietnam. There will be fifteen chapters, one for each month he was there. He had come as far as March 1, 1968, when he stopped. "I felt like I had to clear it with Dan and Rudy first." So he went to the memorial alone on the night of February 28 and stayed until two in the morning on March 1.

"I felt like they were alive. What I sensed of them seemed peaceful and glad. Glad that I had come to say good-bye and hello. I felt welcome at the wall, like they were waiting for me. It was peaceful. I didn't hear words, they didn't say anything, I could just feel it. It is like hearing the enemy in the jungle, that same kind of back-of-the-neck feeling. They let me know they were there if I ever needed them."

He hadn't planned to leave a letter—he had brought a few of his poems with him to place at the memorial—but after he left the wall he had a need to keep talking. "The letter felt like the letter I'd never written to their families." He knew that letters left at the wall were saved, and he thought, "If I couldn't speak to Dan and Rudy's moms, I could speak to other moms."

The next morning he took his wife and three daughters with him to the memorial and he left his letter at the base of Panel 42 East. Then he and his family went to Arlington Cemetery, to the grave of his father, who died two years after Dan got back from Vietnam. He left a letter at Arlington, too, in which he said, "I never really understood what was behind that faraway look in your eyes. Then I went to Vietnam, and I knew, because I had the same look in my eyes. I knew your wars lay heavily on your soul, as did my war. I have begun to find more peace with mine in the last few years, and I wanted you to know that."

Dan Doyle describes one particular night when he stood in the tree line just opposite the apex of the memorial. Several of the lights at the base were out. The center of the memorial was like the entrance to a tunnel. "It looked like a hole going into the earth. There wasn't something I could actually hear, it wasn't auditory, but I felt like I was being called into this hole in the ground. I wasn't being pulled in, but I wasn't repelled, either. I felt welcome. There were so many voices but they were all joined as one. Maybe the peace I felt then is that I know I will join them when I die, and that it's a peaceful place. I didn't want to jump into it, it was more like a window. But it was a place where I knew that I belonged."

GARY G. WRIGHT

Colonel, U.S.A.F., 11th Tactical Reconnaissance Squadron
NOVEMBER 20, 1930–JANUARY 17, 1967
Missing in Action

Dear Daddy,

I wanted to come and see you and bring Heidi and the children to see you, too. Andrea found a small flower and we put it up by your name.

It's been over eighteen years now that you've been missing, and I wish I knew what really happened. I know that I've been lied to about it. It will be seven years ago tomorrow since Mom passed away, but I know that if you are no longer here, then you and she are together and she is at last at peace.

I have a lot of trouble providing for my own family now due to my injuries, but I am trying. I just wish Vietnam had never happened to us. It's hard to explain how the Vietnam vets are treated. They try to make me believe that the pain is all in my mind. They could care less.

I loved and still do love both of you so very much, but for now, I can only remember that love and hope for a day sometime when we can all be together again. If I could only turn back the hands of time for just one day . . .

> *I love you,*
> *Your son,*
> *Gene*

---•---

O N ONE WRIST, Gary Gene Wright, Jr., wears an MIA bracelet with his father's name on it, and on the other, a watch that says "Vietnam Vet and Proud of It." He is a big, burly man with dark hair and dark eyes whose life has been shadowed in two ways by the Vietnam War. In 1967, when Gary was ten, his father, Colonel Gary G. Wright, an Air Force pilot, was shot down over Vietnam. And eight years later, when Gary was himself serving on a Navy ship off Vietnam, he suffered the back injuries that have partially disabled him.

• • •

His Dad had always wanted to be a pilot. When he was about ten or twelve years old and living near a naval base in San Diego, he saw a plane crash on a training mission. He went home and told his mother that when he grew up, he was going to take the place of the pilot who died, and that's what he did.

He was on his way, literally, to the Korean War when he fell in love with a woman who worked behind one of the airline counters at San Francisco International Airport. Gary Wright delayed his departure for Korea by a few days and married her. As soon as he came home, they started a family.

Gary junior was their second child. Three more, including a set of twins, followed. The family lived at Air Force bases in Georgia, Texas, and Arizona, and in 1963, they moved to England.

Gary junior looked up to his dad and loved their special times together. "My brother and I slept in bunk beds. My dad would come in at night, after my brother had gone to sleep, and he'd sneak me out into the living and dining area and let me sit there and build models with him or watch him do his paintings, or sometimes we'd watch a movie. He did that a lot with me. It meant a lot to me because he was always so busy during the day. He bought a motorcycle when we were in England and sometimes we'd ride into the town and get fish and chips and bring them back." His father played the guitar and sometimes he would gather his five children together and sing songs like "On Top of Old Smokey" and "The Big Rock Candy Mountain."

As far as Gary remembers, there never was any tension in his home until his dad started talking about going to Vietnam. He didn't have to go; he chose to, because he wanted to stay with the men in his squadron. Then Gary became aware for the first time of his parents' arguing. "The normal flow of family life just wasn't there." Once, when Gary wanted to go out and play with friends, his mother told him, "Spend more time with your father; he might not be around much longer."

The family had moved back to San Francisco when it came time to say good-bye. They all trooped out to the airport to see Gary senior off. "I remember distinctly the night he left. My dad came and went an awful lot because he was always going to school, but we knew there was something different. He said good-bye to me and he went down the walkway and he looked back and I knew he was crying." Gary promised his dad that he would help take care of his mother.

The moment is chiseled in his memory. "When you lose someone like that, your mind traces back to the last little while together and you really hold that moment in your mind. I remember very vividly that evening in the airport. I wonder if there was anything else I could have said."

Gary was ten years old and in the fifth grade when his dad's plane crashed. At the end of the day he was called to the principal's office and told that his dad was missing. When he got home, the Air Force officers were with his mother. He wasn't worried. "I thought the Air Force was the greatest thing in the world. I knew they would find him."

His mother was pregnant with twins when his dad disappeared. She miscarried. The military doctors who examined her in later years described her as a woman "unable to cope with her grief." She was deeply depressed, and in Gary's words, she "found a friend in the bottle."

The happy part of his childhood was over. Gary and his brother were on their own emotionally. Their mother found it easier to cope with her daughters than with her sons. Gary remembers that when his younger brother had nightmares he would crawl into his bunk and sleep with him.

Over the next few years, the situation went from bad to worse. Gary, who had dreamed of going to the Air Force Academy, did poorly in school. Sisters and brothers did not get along. Drinking and depressed, his mother would sometimes lash out at him. Once he had to go to the hospital for stitches in the back of his head. Gary and his brother went to live with their grandparents for a while.

When he was seventeen, Gary's mother signed the forms so that he could enter the Navy. He was determined to have a career in the service, even if it wasn't in the Air Force. Gary was stationed off the coast of Vietnam on the USS *Oriskany* from 1973 to 1975. He worked on air crews, loading ordnance onto planes and working on maintenance. Although he was not in combat, he injured himself—his back appears to have been permanently damaged by the lifting and heaving—and he receives a small disability payment. Some mornings it takes him an hour to get going—twenty minutes to inch his way out of bed, assisted by his wife, and another forty minutes creaking around the house, trying to straighten up. One doctor told him he may have degenerative arthritis. Like so many vets, he has found the VA better at doling out tranquilizers and pain pills than at diagnosis and treatment.

He decided in the Navy that he did not want a military career.

Since then he has had a series of jobs that seem to end abruptly for one reason or another. "I have a lot of problems with other people. Most of the time, I really don't think it's me. I really don't.

"If it weren't for my wife and kids, I would have headed for the mountains a long time ago by myself and just said the hell with everything." At thirty-one, he is a disappointed and disillusioned man.

"We're not the quote unquote Yuppie generation," says Heidi, Gary's wife, "but we could have been. We're the group that wound up either going to war or protesting the war while the children of the politicians and higher-ups, well, their fathers bought them out of the war and into colleges and they were able to get a good education and go on, and they are the ones that are living in the $250,000 homes and driving Volvos or BMWs."

Heidi has her B.A. and is two years into a master's degree in education, but with three small children, it isn't easy and she's had to put off further study.

Their eldest child, Amanda, is six and profoundly retarded. She is a fine child with blond hair and exquisite blue eyes who moves with a strange energy she seems barely able to control. The other two children are Andrea, five, and Gene, four.

The family lives in a rent-subsidized apartment in McLean, Virginia, and gets by with Gary's disability payments and what they can eke out from part-time jobs. Heidi works in a nearby mall when the children are all in school and Gary earns a small stipend manning a POW/MIA booth set up near the Vietnam Veterans Memorial. There is no leisure time. Says Heidi, "We learned to survive by taking it one day at a time. You make it through one day and, hey, you make it through the next day. We depend on each other, we draw the energy from each other 'cause that's all we've got. There isn't anyone else for us to depend on."

Gary has done what he can to wrest information about his father's case from the military. He thinks there is a good chance his dad survived the crash of his unarmed reconnaissance plane. He was flying low, under radar, eighteen miles south of Hanoi when he was hit by ground fire. "The government has played games with this thing. The Reagan administration has been exceptionally good at pacifying the families. How? They say this is a matter of highest national priority, and the majority of people believe it." Gary feels that the government must make a greater effort to trace reports of live POWs. He believes many are still alive.

The Vietnam Veterans Memorial has both political and personal significance for Gary Wright. It is the focus for his work on the POW/MIA issue, and it is where he connects with his dad. His children know it's the place where they go "to see Grandpa." Gary holds them up to kiss his name.

Although he is at the memorial several times a week to work, he goes to his father's panel far less frequently because it is so wrenching. "When I go down there, I start to walk down the path and the further I get, I feel as though I have this weight on my chest. My breathing changes and my legs feel heavy and I get down in front of my dad's panel and I kind of talk to him. I tell him how the kids are doing and think back to the things we did together. But the hardest thing for me, overall, is the uncertainty. That's there every day—the emotional highs and lows are constant over the years, and for as long as that remains, I can't ever really live a normal life."

Dear Nick,

The little baby you never saw turned 17 in August. She looks like Scotty now; she used to look like you when she was younger.

This was all such a waste. Maybe your sacrifice means this won't happen again.

Dan

The Wall

I miss my friends whose names are here
The times we shared, the laughs and fear
I'm still surprised my name isn't here!
There's Cobb whose date they've got wrong
Wiskey and Logan who died near Tri Bong
"We got to get out of this place," our favorite song.
After 18 years I still can't forget what we did,
*   what we saw*
We fought for our country, but our country
*   screwed us all*
I am sorry my name's not on "the Wall."

Huey
68–69

CLIFFORD EUGENE BENCH

Specialist Four, Troop D, 1st Squadron, 10th Cavalry,
1st Field Force
May 28, 1952–March 16, 1971

Oh, Eugene, my friend, how I remember the good days when we were so young. We played on the same block, we went to the same school. But after graduation you went to the Army and I never saw you again. I've missed you, my friend. I saw your name on the wall. I felt you with me. I felt all of you with me. I left you my crew hat and my jungle shirt. Just look at it and 'member me, cause brother, I remember you. 'Till we meet again, broman.

Herb Neeland

———————•———————

H E WAS always the smallest kid, the one that everyone picked on, but he was my buddy, always," says Herb Neeland. "I was a bigger kid, the sheriff's kid, so I was intimidating. I used to whup their asses and say 'Leave Eugene alone.' He was the slowest, the gawkiest, and he turned out the bravest."

They were hardly a matched set—Herbie, big and rowdy; Gene, gentle and shy. Herb was slick, he knew the moves, and he always made sure Gene was protected. After school they would hang out together at the Cambridge, Ohio, jail, which Herb's dad ran and the family lived above. "We had a lot of fun around the jailhouse," Herb says. "We used to talk to the prisoners through the fence. We'd go down and visit Mrs. Schlosser, she was the cook for the jail, and she used to give us leftovers, some soup beans and white bread."

Gene changed high schools midway through, so he and Herb would meet up at the King Pin Bowling Alley. "It was one of the roughest damn places that you would ever want to walk through," says Herb. "You'd walk in and just kind of excuse yourself from being hit by a beer bottle."

Because they were in different schools, Gene and Herb had started to grow apart. Gene didn't finish high school. He enlisted in the Army, which stationed him in Germany, and then he decided to volunteer for Vietnam. It was in the King Pin Bowling Alley that Herbie saw him for the last time. "The part that hurt me most was that he ignored me, kind of," Herb says. "He was in his uniform and looking great and he was with other kids in uniform, guys he had been in school with." Herb wanted to hug him and say good-bye, but the King Pin Bowling Alley wasn't the place for anything mushy.

Gene was in Vietnam for three months before he was killed. The awkward boy that no one wanted on his team was awarded the Silver Star, the country's third-highest medal. According to the Army, his platoon was moving down a trail when Gene and a medic spotted an NVA soldier in the bushes. At great risk, they tried to capture him and were fired upon from another direction. Gene was shot in the head.

When he learned of Eugene's death, Herb had just joined the Air Force. Because he had just finished basic, he was not able to go to the funeral. It wasn't a coincidence that Gene's death marked the beginning of a traumatic period in Herb's life—a fifteen-year ordeal of booze, pills, dope, and other drugs.

Herb had enlisted in the Air Force to avoid being drafted. His hopes of becoming an air traffic controller were dashed—he was trained to be a medic. His first assignment was in a neurosurgical intensive care unit, where many of his patients were eighteen and nineteen years old and were coming back from Vietnam paralyzed from the neck down. Herb was assigned to the night shift, which seemed to be when most patients died. Getting stoned was the best escape he could find. "It was any pill I could get hold of," he says. "I saw too much death."

Despite his growing drug addiction, the Air Force sent him to Southeast Asia, where he was stationed on a base in Udorn, Thailand. "I didn't spend a sober day in country," he says. "The speed over there, the white horse, is what I took to go to work. I'd smoke a rail, that's one of these, a cigarette, loaded with smack, at least an eighth of a gram." After work at the hospital there would be scotch and grass.

By the time of Herb's tour, in 1973, most of the Vietnam fighting was being done by Asians, whom Herb would help patch up and then send out again. As a sideline, he ran a scam in which he provided doped-up soldiers with clean urine samples so they could pass drug tests. The specimens came from the lifers, who happily provided them in exchange for the druggies' liquor ration cards. Herb called it Operation Golden Flow. This too was a diversion from death. Herb also had to work in the morgue, a job that earned him the nickname Ghostman and deepened his drug addiction. Besides soldiers, Herb handled civilians, such as an Australian woman who had been killed when her tour bus was blown up. To preserve the body Herb had to pack it in ice because frequent power outages made the morgue refrigerators unreliable. It was a wretched experience, worsened by the fact that the dead woman reminded Herb of his mother.

He finally came home in 1974, off heroin, but still on other drugs. His parents met him at the airport and took him to a White Castle, where he ate twenty-one hamburgers, one for each year he'd been alive.

Later, as Herb slid deeper into depression, he realized that his buddy Gene was still on his mind—and in his dreams. "I was on the outside looking in," he says. "It was always like I couldn't get to him. I had a chance to help him and I couldn't."

Eventually, Herb enrolled in nursing school, where he was a B student. Years of practice had made him adept at hiding his addiction, which now involved mainly pills and pot. He fell in love with a nursing supervisor named Carolyn; they married and set up household in Tyler, Texas, with her three sons from a previous marriage. When their own son was born, Carolyn had natural childbirth, but Herb needed twenty-five Tylenol 3 tablets to stay by her side.

It was shortly after the birth of his son that Herb decided to go to the Vietnam Veterans Memorial. This was the beginning of his catharsis; something inside him said, Go there, go there. His wife took $1,300 from the bank and gave it to him with her blessings. "You just go up there and heal yourself," she told Herb. "Have some drinks, talk to some people—this is your time."

He packed his fatigue jacket and hat, and also a hundred Tylenol 3 tablets and a cough-medicine bottle filled with gin. Before he got on the plane he took some pills and smoked a joint. "I was so excited, it was like, Hey, Herb Neeland is going up there to feel better. I had my best cowboy hat on, my brand-new boa-constrictor boots, I was so proud of myself, I looked good, I felt good. I was high as a kite, but it was also that idea of going to the wall, of making peace with Eugene."

He checked into a downtown hotel that night and went to a bar across the street. He stayed there until two in the morning, drinking Beefeater martinis with a vet who had come from Alaska, also to go to the wall. By the time Herb went to the memorial the following morning, he was scared and strung-out from the night before. "The closer I got to the wall, the more sick I got," he remembers. "Where the wall is real small, I just cried out, 'Eugene!' But I never felt so *not* alone. All of a sudden I had five people around me, hugging me, stroking me. They got me over to a bench and said, 'Don't talk, just cry.' I must have cried for an hour."

When Herb was finally ready, he looked for Eugene's name. He went down to the panel, found the name, then left his letter and the jungle hat and shirt. He spent a total of six hours there. "I talked to him about all the things that happened when we were kids," Herb says. "I talked to him about how funny his ears were." He had the sense that Gene understood. In the gray drizzle of the day he felt his friend telling him, "Herb, man, it's okay. It's okay." Someone gave Herb a flower and he left that for Eugene, too.

He flew back to Tyler, Texas, feeling better, unaware that his visit to the wall would set off a maelstrom of despair. Suddenly, there was insomnia, nightmares, and increased drug addiction. He finally cracked on May 5, 1985.

It was just after the tenth anniversary of the fall of Saigon. Herb was home alone with his two-year-old son, watching Howard Cosell interview Rocky Blier, the former football star who had part of his foot blown off in Vietnam, about his war experiences. "I just couldn't take it anymore," Herb says. "I was real bitter." Rocky Blier had managed to return and resume his playing career. Herb thought of Eugene and the other men he knew who didn't come back. What about them?

The rest of that day, he drank and took pills. He finished a half gallon of vodka, and he took fifteen Talwin, a painkiller. After he managed to change and feed his son, he took his M-16 and walked the perimeter of his property. Helicopters were flying overhead, part of a military reserve training program. Herb didn't know where he was. He became so scared that he called a vet hotline number and talked to an ex-Marine, but he wouldn't reveal where he lived.

When his wife came home, she took him back to the psychiatric hospital where she worked and had him admitted. He stayed there for the next month.

For the first time in fifteen years, he went through drug withdrawal. He was treated for PTSD, post-traumatic stress disorder. And while he was a patient, he thought of the memorial. The patience, kindness, and love that the volunteers and vets had shown him there was now part of his healing. "I knew that someone, outside my wife and kids, loved me enough to touch me," he says. "Just knowing there were people like that on this earth was comforting."

Life has come into focus for Herb. He hasn't taken a pill in two years. He has gone back to work at the hospital, and he now wants to return to college and study psychology. He got a violin for Christmas and is learning to play it. He has found that he can think of Eugene and be content.

"Everybody has a special friend they remember from when they were a kid and he was mine," says Herb. "There was a gentleness to him, a real gentleness. My first thought is the playground at school and I remember him smiling when he saw me. I just really loved that kid. We were just two peas in a pod. Every time I saw him, I felt something in my heart. It brings me peace now. A lot of weight has been lifted from my shoulders."

I don't remember the names, only the young faces. I feel guilt for failing so often, but finally I feel pride that I tried. What does anyone know at 19?

I've wanted to come for years. I wasn't ready, too many mixed emotions.

I love you all. I'll never forget you.

Never.

Jeannie Harden
Sgt. USAF 1968–1970
Medic/O.R.

To Kenneth Grant Stoker and Ronald Edward Stoker

In a country you didn't know
With a language you didn't speak
Over causes you didn't understand
By an enemy you often couldn't see
You died for us.
Leaving those that you did love
And this land that you did cherish
And the government that tried to forget
And the people who wouldn't let them
You live for us
In our hearts
For Ever.

Peter Stoker
London, England

JAMES ALEXANDER DAUGHERTY

Corporal, Headquarters & Service Company,
2nd Battalion, 1st Marine Regiment, 1st Marine Division
July 10, 1946–May 9, 1968

I write this letter to you, father, the one who I never knew. People at times comment that I resemble you. But I know not. You never saw me; I never saw you. Sad, is it not? Stranger still is this. I was born March 9, 1968. You knew of the birth of your son, Chadwick J. Daugherty.

But you, father, who had given life, died two months later on May 9, 1968.

I think you would be proud of my accomplishments that I have made so far. They are many for a young person of 17.

Dear father, you shall always be remembered.

> *Your loving son,*
> *Chadwick James Daugherty*

------●------

FOR A college writing assignment Chad Daugherty described finding his father's name on the Vietnam Veterans Memorial:

The rows of names looked like one large mass of confusion. "Where was it?" he silently said. Name after name continued; they never stopped. They became a blur as the teenager tried to find that certain name. Finally admitting his own folly, he went to the directory book on the right side of the Memorial and looked up the name. He memorized the panel number and stared at the date of death, that was only two months after his birth, to the day.

Back down the path he went, past the sixties and fifties, until he reached panel number fifty-seven. Towards the center, at the right edge, he spied the name he sought; his father's name. As his fingers brushed over the name, James Alexander Daugherty, a sad smile formed on the youth's face and a tearful look appeared in his eyes.

From his heart rose a feeling he just could not explain. It only seemed to occur at that place while gazing at the name and dark reflections in the wall. The feeling seemed to torture the heart. Contrasting emotions of love and hate; happiness and sorrow; pride and shame were all felt at once. Why did he put himself to this torture, he wondered? There was no reason to come. No one made him come. Yet he came willingly. He had made the pilgrimage without anyone's knowledge. He had made it because he wanted to.

At the time, in 1986, Chad was a college freshman whose deepest yearning was to learn more about his father. All he knew about the death of the man who gave him life was that he was killed in a trench by a mortar in 1968. But like a determined archeologist, Chad has been piecing together an image of his dad because he desperately wants to know what the two of them might have had in common.

Chad's mother, Norma Gilbert, says that after he received his draft notice, Jim Daugherty joined the Marines because that would delay his departure for the service. They were married in July 1966, and two months later he was on his way to Vietnam. He did not want to go. "All that he ever wanted was to have a family and provide for them." They dreamed of owning their own home near the auto-body-repair shop where Jim planned to work when he came home.

His wife remembers mailing him packages of fudge. He wrote to her that Vietnam would be a beautiful country if it could ever be at peace. He was thrilled when he learned he had a son and eager to get home and see him.

Norma remarried when Chad was small, and she never told him very much about his father. Until very recently, Chad was hesitant to ask. "When my mom learned of my father's death," he says, "she was very upset and threw away anything that had to do with the wedding, wedding pictures, the gown, everything." As a child, Chad was haunted by fantasies that his father would return. "It was like an inside hope, an inner dream, that maybe they identified the wrong body, maybe he will come back and we'll discover all these things we have in common," he remembers. "I'd be wishing he would come back, pop up out of nowhere, get freed from Vietnam as a prisoner of war. I'd think it would be great, and then I'd think of the problems for my mother with two husbands."

His grandparents were quite elderly and Chad saw them infrequently. Although he never learned much about his dad from them while they lived, their deaths, ironically, opened many doors. When the contents of their small home were auctioned off, relatives sent Chad a big box of his father's things. The package arrived on Chad's eighteenth birthday. Its contents were a revelation, as was a visit to the auction itself. "I was trying to find out how he was in comparison to me," Chad says. "I found an old model car that he had never finished—so I could say definitely he was into models. He also seemed to be pretty good in things having to do with his hands—he made some crafts in woodshop; he may not have been too good with the measurements, but it wasn't too bad. It was a lot better than I could have done."

Chad also saw pictures of his parents' wedding and discovered what a beautiful bride his mother had been. In letters he found, he read of his father's romantic feelings for his mother. Even more comforting was a letter that said, "Tell Chad his Daddy loves him."

It is at the Vietnam Veterans Memorial that Chad has found the chance to tell his father of his achievements—his Eagle Scout God and Country Award, his participation in an exchange program in the Latin American country of Colombia, his education. James Daugherty, the youngest of eight children of a Pennsylvania truck farmer, was the first person in his family to graduate from high school. And Chad, an intense, purposeful young man, knows his father would be very proud to find him in college today, as a freshman at Indiana University, not far from Pittsburgh. Chad will be the family's first college graduate, an education paid for by the death benefits of a father he never knew.

Of the memorial Chad says, "It's the one place in the world where I feel as if I am given the opportunity to communicate with my father and tell him how much I love him and respect him and wish we could have shared a life together." Its black color is appropriate, he feels, since the memorial represents to him the blank spaces the soldiers' deaths left in the lives of those who miss them. "It's a place of healing where those affected immediately by the war, and future generations, can go and see exactly what the human price of war is and understand the anguish of those left behind."

He got the idea to write a note to his dad when he saw a letter someone else had left at the memorial. As he explained in his college composition:

He looked down at his feet and the path. A clear plastic covered letter caught his attention. He knelt to read it. Who wrote the letter was not important, the meaning was. Someone had lost a loved one and felt the need to say something that was once unsaid or to reiterate what was common knowledge. Whatever be the case, the letter meant "I love you and I miss you" to one of the names on the wall.

The letter was short and the youth stood and continued on his way when he finished it. Abruptly he halted. Should he write one? he thought. "No, that would be foolish," he said out loud. He continued to think, now silently. No one would understand. Anyway, he couldn't say . . . Why couldn't he? It really wouldn't matter. He had paper and pen. He didn't have to tell anyone and he could write a letter in no time at all.

The youth went back and re-traced his steps to panel fifty-seven. By the far side of the path he knelt, got his paper, pen and notebook and began to write. After two lines he stopped. They didn't reflect how he felt. They weren't his true feelings. He crumpled the paper and began to write anew on a fresh clean sheet of paper. His pen didn't stop now, the words and feelings flowed true. After he finished re-reading the letter, he laid it at the base of number fifty-seven, stood up and without another look, he hurried in the direction he came from.

McFarland,

To watch you die has been the most painful encounter of my life. I prayed for you, my brother of war. When I turned my head in helplessness your breath of life had stopped. I could no longer hear your breathing then. I knew that you were at peace. Bless you, for you are the hero.

Houston, Texas
January 1985

Dear Guale (Wally):

For the past nineteen years, I have been thinking about you and how it would have been if you and I would have reunited after your tour in Nam. I was in Okinawa when I learned of your death and needless to say, I was shocked and saddened.

Upon learning of your death, as I do today, I recalled our teenaged days when we were migrant workers in Michigan and Ohio. I specifically remember Nacha, your mother, and how she treasured your presence. You, unlike me, were her oldest son and because of this she had high hopes for you and your family. You may recall when we were picking cherries that she constantly commented that she looked forward to the day when she would not have to work in the fields because you as her "hijo" would be able to finish high school and in turn you would help your parents overcome the poverty under which we all lived.

From Mom, I learned that you had barely achieved the goal that your mother had for you when you were called to serve. As you know, I was already in the service at this time and we really never had a chance to see each other before you went to basic training. I remember telling Mom that I was sure that we would be able to trade war stories once the two of us were discharged. How wrong I was and I still lament the fact that you weren't able to share some of your last words with your family and those of us who had grown up with you in the migrant fields.

Today, I am here in Washington on a business trip and I came to the monument to personally tell you and others that my family and I sincerely appreciate what you were able to do for us before God called you to his kingdom. Knowing your childhood background, I know that you demonstrated exemplary behavior as a soldier. Moreover, I have reason to believe that you died at a moment when you were giving it your best to protect those who fought adjacent to you.

Finally, I want to say that because of your mother's desire for you, I believe that should you have returned able-bodied you would have done the same thing I did upon discharge. Since then I have attended *college and over six years ago I obtained my terminal degree. I now work as an administrator at a major university in Texas. Though I have been successful in my post Vietnam endeavors, I cannot help but continue thinking of the many guys, like yourself, who died before they actually began to live. You and others listed in the monument are my heroes and I want you to know it!*

May God Bless You!

Con Respecto y Amor
Enrique

RICHARD CLAYTON EWALD

Private First Class, Company C, 1st Battalion,
27th Infantry Regiment, 25th Infantry Division
MARCH 24, 1947–OCTOBER 29, 1968

Hi Lover!

Seventeen years . . . you're still twenty-one—forever young, but gone. Murdered. And nothing will make your loss to us less of a tragedy.

The first gray hairs sneak onto my head as I face thirty-seven. I look into the eyes of my teenage son and I wonder—have we done enough to change things . . . have we done enough . . .

Waddaya say, kid—I brought you flowers. I always brought you flowers, didn't I? Picked from the neighbors' yards on the way to the school bus . . . It's how we fell in love. And then I gave you daisies in the midst of all those white slabs of death.

Your slab said they gave you a purple heart—for dying. Well, this here letter is a purple heart for living. I thought it might mean more to you. The paper is a gift from my daughter—she loves purple. She's 10 and ¾ years old and beautiful, and someday she'll have a first love too. I hope he has your kindness and humor. And when she's thirty-seven and still looking for some of those answers, I hope they can touch one another and talk of how they've changed and say thanks for having been a part of my life when everything still lay ahead.

It was important for me to come today . . . to touch your name on the wall that makes it all real . . . I'm still trying to say goodbye. I never managed that very well with us, did I? But you made all of that OK and that made a big difference in my life. The only way I've ever known to pay you back for that gift is to live my life as if it mattered and to work every day in every way for what is right.

Oh, it was wonderful to be in love the Spring of '65. That part of you will always be alive—love doesn't divide, it multiplies. And the me I bring to the wonderful life and love I share with Dick and our precious, precious children is a me that is a part of you.

I'll always bring you flowers. You gave me love. Goodbye. Hello.

Carole Ann

THEY MET in the back row of the band. She played the drums, he played the tuba.

Carole Wedding was a junior and the new girl at Hopkins High School in a Minneapolis suburb. Gradually, their shy and humorous friendship grew into first love. All that year, they had band every morning in first period. Carole picked blossoms on her way to the school bus and brought them to Rick. "I was always bringing him flowers," she says. "It just got to be a real joke. I don't remember how it started or why I started doing it, but I remember the other kids walking to the bus teasing me about it."

Because they were a year apart, band was the only class they shared, so the rest of the day they passed notes to each other when they met in the hallways. He always began his notes to her with "Hi Lover," but not for the reason one might suspect. "He said I was a person who had a lot of love for everybody and everything," she says. "It was a view of myself that I hadn't had before; that I was a person who gave love to other people and was there for them."

They played miniature golf together, double-dated with Dick and Georgine, talked on the phone incessantly, went on band trips, and sat and talked in his car at the end of her street. They continued dating throughout the summer; when Carole went off alone on a camping trip with her parents, she picked wildflowers and mailed them to Rick. "There I was on this beautiful island in the middle of nowhere and all I'm doing is talking to my dog and writing to Rick."

Rick left for St. Cloud State College in the fall and gave Carole his high school ring with the burgundy stone. By the end of October, though, she decided to give it back. She cared about him as a friend, but her feelings had changed and she decided to break off their relationship. Telling him was one of the hardest things she had ever had to do.

He accepted her decision with grace, they remained friends, wrote regularly, and even saw each other every now and then. Carole has never forgotten that Rick forgave her and remained kind to her though she had hurt him.

After attending college for about a year, Rick came back to Minneapolis to work until he was drafted into the Army. His brother, Bob, says Rick had a matter-of-fact attitude about going to Vietnam: "I think it was something he knew had to be done and he would do it the best he could."

Carole remembers that Rick made her promise to write him in Vietnam, and she agreed. But during the next nine months, she never heard from him. Then it was too late. "I was home, the last weekend in October, studying downstairs," Carole recalls. "My mom came down and handed me the newspaper. There was a row of faces and stories and there was Rick. That's how I found out he died."

Rick was the point man for his platoon when they were ambushed. He provided a spray of fire so his buddies could take cover. He was shot in the stomach and died of pneumonia in a hospital two days later. The Army awarded him the Silver Star.

For Carole, Rick's death marked the end of a cataclysmic year, 1968: Tet, the Martin Luther King and Robert Kennedy murders, the Democratic Convention in Chicago. And when, the week before her twentieth birthday, Carole heard that the boy she thought too gentle to be a soldier had died, it seemed that everything good her generation had believed in had "got lost in assassinations and the horror and mud of Vietnam."

Carole stayed at St. Olaf College the day Rick was buried. It was the day of the first snowfall, and she remembers how hard she cried. She found a friend and simply talked about Rick—and then she stopped talking about him for more than a decade; she kept him inside. "He gave me love and a sense of myself at a point in my life when it made a real difference," she says. "His death, and all of the deaths, seemed so senseless, so unnecessary. I came away from it saying, 'This is unacceptable'; I'd have to do something to try to make things better."

A few years later, Carole married Dick Page, a man she met at college; he enlisted in the Air Force after finishing dental school and they were stationed at McCord Air Force Base in Washington. Carole worked on her master's degree in human relations, avoiding the military world. As part of her studies, she worked in a veterans' hospital, but she never talked to anyone about Rick.

After her husband completed his stint in the Air Force, the couple moved to Eugene, where they live today with their two children. Carole finds the political activism of their Oregon community congenial. "I want the world to exist and be a place that can be home for everybody, home in the best senses of the word, of food and shelter, love and peace," she says. "I want people to live together and not destroy each other or destroy the whole earth."

On a trip back to Minneapolis in 1979 Carole went to visit Rick's grave in a military cemetery. She brought daisies and sat there for several hours. When she heard about the Vietnam Veterans Memorial, she sensed she finally might be able to say good-bye.

She visited the memorial with her husband and children in October 1985, almost seventeen years after Rick's death. It was a gray and rainy day. Carole bought a bouquet of carnations by the entrance to a subway station to leave by his name.

"We walked the whole length of it, and it feels like you almost go down into it, it's so all-encompassing," she says. "It makes the war and the loss and the people so real."

When she finally found Rick's name she talked about him to her children. Then "I spent some time talking inside myself with Rick; it was the most natural thing in the world." After being alone by Rick's panel for a while, she sat down on a bench with her husband and cried.

Before leaving Washington, Carole returned to the memorial with her family and left her letter at the base of Panel 40 West. She had brought the letter with her from Eugene, because she had the sense, even before she got there, that this "was the place to find Rick again.

"I can imagine that we would have been very different people, but I know we would always have been friends. Rick would always have been somebody I could have talked to; there have been times when I really wanted to talk to him about who we were then and the way things are now. One of the things that was important for me to say at the memorial was to let him know what a difference it's made in my life that he forgave me for hurting him and was my friend. He wasn't bitter about it and didn't blame me for it. I always hoped he had another love in his life, but I never did know."

There is a lot she doesn't know but would like to know about the last year of Rick's life. None of their mutual friends heard from Rick after he went to Vietnam. She has felt hesitant about approaching his mother. She hopes that someday she will find someone who served with Rick in the Army and will be able to fill in a gaping hole in her life.

Not long ago, Carole made another pilgrimage to honor Rick Ewald. The touring replica of the Vietnam Veterans Memorial—exactly half the size of the original with all the 58,132 names on its black panels —came to Eugene and drew 50,000 visitors during its week-long stay. The first night, hundreds stood in a driving rain that quickly turned the grassy park around the memorial into mud that wheezed when you stepped into it. The crowd huddled underneath umbrellas as the names of those killed in Vietnam from the area were read off. Carole Page came that night, as she would every other night.

That first evening, she had brought chrysanthemums from a neighbor's yard and a small Styrofoam cup with sand in it so it would hold a candle. She lit the candle that night and came back every night with a fresh one.

On the next to the last day, she left a note for Rick. She did not expect to get back again. But her plans changed and on the final evening, she found herself there one last time. At the base of Rick's panel was an envelope addressed to "Carole."

She held it by the candlelight. Then she walked away and leaned against a lamppost and read the unsigned note:

Dear Carole,

I did come home in the hearts and the minds of each of the living. Every man and woman that came back brought a part of me. I have talked to you with their voices and loved you with their hearts. Don't be scared for I am always with you. I will always be there in the still of the night. Be still, listen, you will hear my voice.

In the silent, almost holy atmosphere, she read it over and over and over again.

Tribute to a Vietnam Vet:

This is a tribute to all of you who died so valiantly, in a war that was not your own; yet you died anyway. I leave this patch as a gift from all of those who were there with you but are yet alive today, to thank you for your sacrifice. I am sad that you had to die but thankful that I (1st Cav combat medic) still live after two tours in the hell that was Vietnam. It is my prayer that today's Army is not called to task. Should they ever be, it is my fervent hope that they will fight as gallantly as those of us who did what the weaker would never dare to do, to walk where those so critical would never be brave enough to walk. To see things that those of lesser character could never bear to see. To feel the putridness of fear in the bowels of your soul, and yet walk on to a mission you did not choose.

May your souls find peace in death, among the highest angels of heaven that did not exist in your last tortured moments upon the earth.

We did what we could but it was not enough because I found you here. All of you are not just names on this wall, you are alive. Your blood's on my hands, your screams in my ears, your eyes in my soul. I told you you'd be alright but I lied. Please forgive me. I see your face in my son. I can't bear the thought. You told me about your wife, your kids, your girl, your mother. Then you died. I should have done more. Your pain is ours. Please, God. I'll never forget your faces. I can't, you're still alive.

My dear son, Rafael A. Chavez:

My son Ralphie:

How I miss you! I want you to talk to me. I think of you every day and every hour of the day and night. If I could hug you and kiss you one more time. Oh Ralphie, how I miss you. There's no words for it.
I love you my son. Be with God and I'll pray for you.

All our love,

Mom
Dad
Amy and Karen

Ed,

Red stains the dirt
Red stains
The fabric of my trousers
Spattered with your life
The warmth dissipating
Even as your torn lungs
Release their final breath—
Its father used in
Warning me to be alert.

Dust devils at my feet now
The terror of your destruction
Close at hand
I turn and fire
To survive
To rent gashes in yellow skin
Like those burned on my eyes.

The battle over, I return in horror
To your last footfall
To see again the witness to my loss of immortality.

But you are gone.
Your remains are drying dust in my memory,
I do not now know if you ever existed.

Winnetka

ALLEN H. ROBERTSON

Warrant Officer, Headquarters and Headquarters Company,
1st Brigade, 1st Cavalry Division (Airmobile)
OCTOBER 6, 1948–JUNE 3, 1969

Dear Allen,

It is that time of year again for me to get to say my special hello to you. I feel so close to you when I am here at "the wall." When I see, feel, and touch your name on this black granite wall, Panel 23 West, Line 57, I feel such pride for having known you during our six years of high school and the three years after, we had nine years of a very special friendship which will never be forgotten and which will be cherished forever. I want to believe that your death was not in vain, but I miss you so, it still hurts having you gone. When I leave "the wall" I leave with an emptiness and a heartache, but I also leave with a great deal of pride. You served your country well and you paid the ultimate price by giving your precious life. When I was told of your death on June 3, 1969, a little of me died with you. Matter-of-fact, I wished that I could have gone down with you when your helicopter was shot down near Saigon on that bleak June day. Many times I ask myself why you died and left me behind? But I will never forget all the good memories I have, like the Homecoming Dance of '65 when you fell on your behind trying to impress me with what a good dancer you were. I still laugh at that memory, but a smile always crosses my face when I think of you.

Remember they called you, me, and Jerry Lynn Noe the Three Musketeers of Rule High School because when you saw one, you saw all three? Well, Jerry's name is down on Panel 22 East, Line 46, you two always did stick together, but you guys left me out this time. I didn't want to be left out of this, either. I don't have to tell you about Jerry being killed in June of 1967 because you guys are walking the streets of Heaven together right now. But you had two more years than Jerry, but for what? Want to know another coincidence? Both of you got killed in June, but two years apart.

I named one of my daughters' middle name after Jerry's middle name, Lynn. Now don't get all flustered, I would have named her after you, but she didn't look like Allen Harvey.

Allen, we had something special and my feelings for you have never faded and I will keep those feelings till the end of time and then through eternity.

The time has come once again for me to leave, but I look ahead to next year when I will be able to come back to our special place at

"the wall." I know you are not lonely because you have Jerry there
and the 58,132 brothers and sisters whose names are on the wall
with you.

Remember till next year, I love and I miss you.

Love you,
Pattye Sampson Taylor
Knoxville, Tennessee

"Greater Love Hath No Man,
Than to Give His Life for God,
America and Fellow Man."
Your Death Is My Tragic Loss
But Heaven's Sweet Gain.

———————•———————

THE Vietnam Veterans Memorial is where Pattye Taylor finds her friends again: Allen Robertson, the good kisser and bad dancer; and Jerry Lynn Noe, the one who could find fun anywhere. "I feel such a sense of freedom there," she says. "I can express myself, and tell the wall how I feel and not have anyone go, 'Oh, God, here she goes again.' No one thinks you're crazy up there."

Pattye's first visit, on Veterans Day, 1984, coincided with the dedication of the memorial's bronze statue of the three infantrymen. She remembers the hundreds of vets milling around. It was like one big family, and guys offered to buy her hot dogs and beer. She remembers one wheelchair-bound black vet from Connecticut who kidded her about her syrupy Southern speech. "You never meet a stranger at the wall," she explains.

It is a place, Pattye has found, "where if you look sad, someone will come up and give you a hug, or pat you on the back." Next to her family, the memorial is what matters most to Pattye. Each fall, for Veterans Day, she makes the trip from Knoxville on a chartered bus. A local vet center sponsors the trip and Pattye and her friends raise money for it with bake sales and car washes. It is the highlight of her year, the only one she can count on.

• • •

Pattye Sampson Taylor's two best friends were killed in the war, two years apart. For ten years, she never spoke about Vietnam or the Three Musketeers of Rule High School, of whom she was the only survivor. She cried, but only when she was alone.

Though she was born in Alabama, Pattye's family moved to Knoxville when she was still a small child. She met Allen Robertson when she was twelve and in the seventh grade; they were in the same homeroom throughout high school and were pictured side by side in every yearbook, except for the time the photo editor didn't know how to alphabetize and accidentally separated them.

Allen was stocky and had light brown hair; he was going to make something of himself. Pattye says he was "quiet, until you got to know him." He played football his freshman and sophomore years of high school, when he wasn't playing in his band, called Junkmen. Jerry Lynn Noe, the third musketeer, was the wild card. The tall, lanky blond cared more about good times than good grades—he knew how to keep the fizz in life. Pattye, Allen, and Jerry were inseparable. They cheered on their team, the Golden Warriors, and went to movies and drive-in restaurants together. When they felt really impetuous, they would play pranks, like hurtling rolls of toilet paper into trees.

But the Three Musketeers, pranksters and pals, were split up during their senior year when Jerry transferred out of Rule High School and then, without graduating from his new school, enlisted in the Army.

His first letter home was also his last. It arrived on his dad's birthday and he apologized for not sending a card. He said Vietnam seemed interesting, and he had already stood guard all night on top of a big tower. Jerry was part of what came to be called the Lost Platoon of the 173rd Airborne Brigade, obliterated during ferocious fighting in the Central Highlands. Three weeks and a day after arriving in Vietnam—a month before his nineteenth birthday—he was dead.

Pattye went to the funeral. There was an open casket with a glass top. Nonetheless, Jerry's death didn't seem real.

She and Allen had graduated from Rule High School earlier that spring. Their high school romance had ebbed back into a close friendship. He started at the University of Tennessee, but after a year or so of college, he enlisted in the Army and went to aviation school to learn how to fly helicopters. Allen had been in Vietnam for ninety-one days when his chopper plummeted into the ground, killing him.

Pattye was married and the mother of two small children when she heard about Allen's death. She had moved back to Alabama with her husband, a truck driver, and she didn't have the money to return to Knoxville for Allen's funeral. Her two golden warriors were gone.

Difficult years followed for Pattye. She was overwhelmed by the relentless demands of two babies and one grown man, and there didn't seem to be any way out. She began to resent her husband, her children, and herself.

But she survived, she got by, and when the family moved to Pensacola in 1979, Pattye decided to do something for herself. She signed up for a course at the local junior college. Her husband thought she was crazy.

There were several Vietnam vets in her first class, and she started to talk to them. It was a natural alliance: the vets had someone who genuinely cared about what they had to say, and Pattye found buddies who "didn't put down my stuff." Her shyness and insecurity began to dissolve.

She remembers the first day she spoke in class. The discussion had turned to the war, and a woman said she thought America owed the Vietnamese reparations for all the damage done to their country. Pattye popped up and said, "Who are you to say we should take funds and give them to the Vietnamese? It was a war we should never have been involved in in the first place." Her vet friends started clapping, and her professor, amazed, said, "You said something out loud!"

Vietnam was back in her life. The war did for Pattye what feminism did for other women of her generation: it gave resonance to her deepest needs and feelings and provided the tools with which to forge an identity.

She and her family moved back to Knoxville, where she became active as a volunteer in the vet center. She did filing and typing and answered the phones. She began to buy and read books about the war, and she now has a collection that would rival that of many small libraries—138 at last count. Her commitment deepened with her knowledge of Vietnam, and she decided to get a college degree so she could work counseling veterans. "It's a way of paying back the guys and the girls who went over there and did what they did," she says. "I wanted to join the service, and I didn't. If I had, I could have gone over to Vietnam too, and done my part."

She saw the memorial for the first time at dawn, after an all-night bus trip from Tennessee. Pattye went first to Panel 23 West to find Allen's name. "I didn't think it would grab me like it did," she says. Her knees got weak, her heart beat faster, and tears came. For the first time in a long, long while she felt his presence. "He was there and I wanted to be there, too. Even though his body is in the ground here in National Cemetery, I don't get the same feeling there, the same inner peace. Maybe it's because all the other names are at the wall."

After that first day, she dreamed about Allen. She saw his helicopter crash and then heard his voice. "He kept telling me it was okay, not to worry, he still loved me." She still dreams frequently of him; usually she's running up to him in Rule High School, hugging him and telling him she's glad he is alive. She has had only one dream that frightened her—Allen was dead but was chasing her, and she ran into a high school locker room to hide.

On her second trip to the wall, the following year, she brought Allen a letter, leaving it in an eight-by-ten frame. "I felt I could talk to him one on one," she says. "It felt like I was talking directly to him and he knew it." She always brings something small for Jerry Lynn Noe, too—the year she left the letter for Allen, she left Jerry a postcard. Now she always leaves flowers for both. These are more than gestures for her; they have become a part of her life. The hardest aspect of her annual visit to the memorial, in fact, is going home.

"I feel like I belong there," she says. "When we get ready to leave, I feel so empty. It's like I'm leaving a part of myself there. That's why I'm so eager to get back from year to year. I find a peace there, a tranquillity, even though it only lasts a short while when I'm home."

July 5, 1985

Dear Lieutenant:

I'm here today with my son, Jim, and my dearest friend, Debbie. It's been fifteen years since I put you, already dying, onto a dustoff. Losing you was so devastating to the platoon because you were so much more than our Lieutenant. You were our leader, our friend, our confidant, our brother, our heart.

Even after I came home I felt responsible for your death since you were hit on one of my squad's tracks, and for the others I'd left when I took a job off the line. I felt I should have been with them. I knew on an intellectual level I wasn't responsible but the guilt that lay in my heart stayed for years.

Finally on Veterans Day, 1979, I went to Arlington Cemetery, sat down and cried out loud "I'm sorry you're dead but I must get on with my life. What do you want?" The answer I got was so swift and strong it was as if it had been spoken. "We are dead but you live and through you we live. Don't let America forget us."

So I've gone to Arlington every Veterans and Memorial Day and went to the ceremonies dedicating this wall and the statue in 1982 and 1984. I've met a lot of very special men. Men America needs.

Last May I went to New York City for the dedication of its Vietnam Veterans Memorial. It was a trip I really didn't want to make but I felt I had to go for you and the others who couldn't. I found not cold-hearted New Yorkers, but Americans who looked you straight in the eye, sometimes with tears, and welcomed us home and thanked us for the sacrifices we'd made. I saw mothers holding up pictures of their precious treasure, their son. Finally America has awakened and taken home those of us who live and remember you and all the others.

I tried so much to keep you alive the day you died and I tried to keep your spirit alive while the country for which you died tried to forget you. At last you live again but not just in the hearts of us who loved you. You live in America's heart as well.

Even people who didn't lose a friend or relative in Vietnam are touched by this wall and those who did lose someone reach out and touch it. My son is just one year old. I've tried to imagine the pain parents feel when they see their son's name here. But the love that develops between men who've fought together, protected each other, bound each other's wounds, and together grieved the loss of another is a very special love.

The memory of you and the loss of you is with me almost every day. I miss you, I love you and I'll never forget you but I don't have to go to dedications, parades or reunions but can now go because I want to. I kept your spirit alive till America woke up, sir. I'm done. Rest well my friend, my Lieutenant.

Sgt. Cass

WILLIAM R. STOCKS

Sergeant, Headquarters and Headquarters Company,
1st Battalion, 6th Infantry, 23rd Infantry Division (Americal)
MAY 9, 1947–FEBRUARY 13, 1969

. . . I am the one who rocked him as a baby. I am the one who kissed away the hurts. I'm the one who taught him right from wrong. I'm the one who held him for the last time and watched him fly away to war. I'm the one who prayed each night "Dear God keep him safe." I'm the goofy mom who sent him a Christmas tree in Vietnam. I'm the one whose heart broke when told my Billy had died in a helicopter crash. And now I'm the one who still cries at night because of all the memories I have that will never die.

Oh, yes, Billy, this mother of yours remembers. I remember the good times and I remember the bad times. But you were so full of life and kept me busy the 21 years I had you, that I now thank God for letting me be your Mom and for leaving me so many more good memories than bad ones. I love you, Billy, and I miss you so.

Mom

———•———

ELEANOR WIMBISH's deepest satisfaction has always come from her family. She is happiest when the beds are full, the screen door slams, and the laughter of children flutters through the house like confetti.

Now the laughter comes from her eight grandchildren, but for many years, it was her Billy who made the house come alive. "He was little Mr. Jerry Lewis, who went through life making other people laugh," she says. "Somebody asked me one time how I remembered my son. I said, 'Laughing.' "

As a girl, Eleanor looked forward to motherhood, and she got an early start. By eighteen, she had quit high school, married, and given birth to a daughter, Donna. For a time she was happy. But when her husband came home from World War II, he seemed changed by the things he had seen but could not talk about. He drank and became abusive. She was scared, and she still blanks out much of that period in her life, which she remembers only as a hell on earth. A short while after Billy was born, in 1947, she left the marriage and moved to Baltimore, to clerk in a department store.

In time, she met Russell Wimbish, a man with clear blue eyes whose childhood polio forced him to rely on a wheelchair. Her mother told her it would never work. That was thirty-two years ago.

Donna and Billy adored their stepfather. Another son was born a few years later and two more daughters followed. Eleanor Wimbish finally had her family and a noisy, happy, hectic household on Ralph Road in suburban Glen Burnie, Maryland.

Billy was in love with life from the word go. Hardly any of his schoolwork can be found in Eleanor's cedar chest because he would wad up his papers and throw them at kids on the way home. "He was the kind that would pinch the girls, then look up at you real innocently and say he didn't do it," remembers his mother. The Boy Scouts were too tame for him. Billy wanted to be outdoors, playing baseball or football or raising his rabbits, Cuddles and Midnight.

He was a smart boy who did not work hard in school. "Many times teachers or the school principal would call me to come in for a conference," Eleanor says. "They would always tell me the same thing: your son is like a millionaire, throwing his money down the drain; Bill spends most of his days telling jokes and showing off to the other students to make them laugh." That was his genius, his mother says, making other people happy.

He left high school before graduation and went to work. After a few odd jobs, he decided to learn the dry-cleaning business. But as the draft began to shadow his life, he enlisted in the Army. He was in Germany, an MP with only a year left in his tour of duty, when he decided to volunteer for Vietnam.

"I begged him not to go," recalls his mother, but his answer was always the same: "Mom, you don't understand. There's a job that's got to be done and I've got to help them do it."

On his last leave before going off to Vietnam, Billy ate and ate. He had a passion for chocolate, and he thought mashed potatoes went with everything. By the time he got to Southeast Asia, he had filled out; his buddies nicknamed him Spanky because his round, jovial face reminded them of *Our Gang*'s hero.

Billy arrived in Vietnam in September 1968; by December he told his parents he was counting the days until he got home. He hated to fly his medevac missions because seeing dead and wounded GIs was so upsetting. "I'll never be so glad to get out of a place in all my life as I will out of here," he wrote. "I guess the people running this war know what they're doing, but I sure don't understand . . . people are getting killed and it just doesn't seem like any progress is being made."

Eleanor had sent her son the usual CARE packages of cookies and fudge, but that Christmas she wanted to do something more. So she packed up and sent a four-foot artificial Christmas tree decorated with unbreakable ornaments and three little monkeys to symbolize his younger siblings. To Billy and his friends, it was like a sequoia. He wrote his mom that he and his buddies sang Christmas carols around it.

Billy usually flew supply missions with the 198th Light Infantry Brigade, which was based in Chu Lai. On February 13, 1969, the chopper he was riding in crashed. Billy, twenty-one years old, died on the day before Valentine's Day, the birthday of Russell Wimbish, the only man he ever called Dad.

Years later, Eleanor Wimbish would write:

> So, Vietnam, what did you take from me? You took my son, Bill. You took part of my hopes and part of my dreams. You broke my heart! You took something from me most people do not even realize they have until they lose it, and that is security. These things and more you took from me when you took my son, Bill. You absolutely changed my life and from then on, nothing was ever the same.

But Eleanor had to pull herself together to meet the needs of her four other children. She had to be strong—she is the sort of woman others lean on when their own strength falters. Though she relied on her husband and her faith, Eleanor survived by working out her deepest pain alone. "When it gets to be too much, and it does sometimes, I have a little corner that I go into and I say, 'God, I just can't handle this load on my shoulders. You're going to have to take a little off.' And he does."

To sustain herself, she turned to writing to Billy. In the early morning hours, when her house was quiet and still, the letters, like her tears, just seemed to flow. Now she leaves them at the Vietnam Veterans Memorial; they're mounted on cardboard, wrapped in plastic, and propped up on slim wooden stands her husband builds.

In one of her first letters to Billy, she described what it was like to be at the memorial on the day it was dedicated, November 9, 1982:

> *The day was unseasonably warm and sunny when we arrived in Washington, D.C. We got out of the car and started walking toward*

this memorial. I could feel the pull toward the black wall, yet my feet didn't want to move. I was so scared. I was afraid I would find your name on this wall, and yet I was afraid some mistake had been made and your name had been left out. So how does one try to explain such mixed emotions? I'll never forget that day as your father and I started looking for your name. We had been looking for about half an hour when your father quietly said, "Honey, here it is." As I looked to where his hand was touching the black wall, I saw your name, William R. Stocks. My heart seemed to stop. I felt as though I couldn't breathe. It was like a bad dream. My teeth chattered. I felt as though I were freezing. God, how it hurt. I looked around at all the people up and down this black wall, this memorial to all those men and women who had lost their lives in Vietnam, these thousands and thousands of names. I reached for your father's hands. They were ice cold. His face was pale. He looked at this black wall and then at me, and said, "What a waste. All these men and women dead, and for what? For fighting a war they had no way of winning."

This was all it took to break me up. The pain of losing you was back in full force. The memories were choking me. How terrible the pain for me, and for all the loved ones of those who had lost their lives in Vietnam. From the wall, like a mirror reflecting my blurred tears, I seemed to see faces. Then I realized it was not the faces of the ones who had died, but of the living who were here like me to find the names of a loved one, to know their loved one was chiseled in granite for all to see until time is no more. In the circle of God, we know where to find you when our turn comes to go. Signed, Mom.

To date, Eleanor has written at least two dozen letters to Billy; they are placed at the memorial on his birthday, Christmas, Veterans Day, Valentine's Day—whenever she misses him a lot. "As I see Bill's name, with all the others, it helps me to know I am not alone in my pain," she says. "When I touch his name, my pain momentarily increases, if you know what I mean, yet it decreases. So what am I trying to say? On this black wall, there is much pain, yet there is much love."

The writing that began to bring her closer to Bill has brought her closer to others. She writes regularly to veterans she has met at the memorial and in the parades she marches in for Bill. She talks, laughs, listens, and cries with them. She loves them and they love her back. One told her, "Maybe God took Billy so you could help all the rest of us."

Eleanor Wimbish will never forget her son and she is determined that the world will not either. She has found a way, through common gestures, to be a quiet force of goodness in the world.

If I could just have the return of one day,
  I wonder which day I would pick?
Would it be the one where they said, "It's a boy,"
  or the day that you took your first step?
Or the day that you first played a Little League game,
  or the day you alone rode your bike?
Or the day that you laughed as you happily said,
  "Got my license, Mom, now can I drive?"

* * * * *

Now I'll not hear you open the door and call out,
  "Mom, I'm home, so what time do we eat?"
But I know that God blessed me when he loaned you to me,
  my Billy, for twenty-one years.
So never again will my arms hold you tight,
  for you've gone to your home in the sky.
So until God calls me to be with you there,
  in my heart you'll be ever alive.

This poem is dedicated to 1st Lt. Sharon Ann Lane, 2nd Lt. Pamela Dorothy Donovan, 1st Lt. Hedwig Diane Orlowski, Capt. Eleanor Grace Alexander, Capt. Mary Therese Klinker, 2nd Lt. Carol Ann Drazba, Lt. Col. Annie Ruth Graham, and 2nd Lt. Elizabeth Ann Jones, eight women nurses who died in Vietnam.

I went to Vietnam to heal
and came home silently wounded.
I went to Vietnam to heal
and still awaken from nightmares
about those we couldn't save.
I went to Vietnam to heal
and came home to grieve for those
we sent home blind, paralyzed,
limbless, mindless.
I went to Vietnam to heal
and discovered I am not God.

To you whose names are on this wall
I am sorry I couldn't be God.
If I were God, if there were a God,
there would be no need for such a wall.

But I am not God, and so I go on
seeing the wounded when I hear a
chopper, washing your blood from my hands,
hearing your screams in my sleep, scrubbing
the smell of your burned bodies from my clothes,
feeling your pain, which never eases,
fighting a war that never ends.

Dusty
Vietnam 1966–68

DUSTY

———•———

SHE WENT TO VIETNAM to heal and came home so wounded that to survive she changed her name, her profession, and her past. She agreed to talk about her experience anonymously. Dusty was her nickname in Vietnam.

"Vietnam cost me a great deal: a marriage, two babies, the ability to bear healthy children, the ability to practice my life's chosen profession, my physical health, and at times, my emotional stability. After the weight of my postwar trauma reached a critical mass, I changed my name, my profession, my residence, and my past. Silence and isolation allowed me to rebuild a life that for years was outwardly normal."

It almost worked. She is a woman of graceful and angular beauty with a mind that cuts through superficiality as a diamond cuts glass. She is married to a businessman who has no idea that his wife was ever a nurse, in the Army, or in Vietnam.

"When you are sitting there working on someone in the middle of the night and it's a nineteen-year-old kid who's ten thousand miles from home and you know that he's going to die before dawn—you're sitting there checking his vital signs for him and hanging blood for him and talking to him and holding his hand and looking into his face and touching his face and you see his life just dripping away and you know he wants his mother and you know he wants his father and his family to be there and you're the only one that he's got, I mean his life is just oozing away there—well, it oozes into your soul. There is nothing more intimate than sharing someone's dying with them. This kid should have had a chance to grow up and have grandkids, he should have had a chance to die in bed with his loving family around him. Instead, he's got this second lieutenant. When you've got to do that with someone and give that person, at the age of nineteen, a chance to say the last things they are ever going to get to say, that act of helping someone die is more intimate than sex, it is more intimate than childbirth, and once you have done that you can never be ordinary again."

As a little girl, she adored science. In high school, her guidance counselor suggested that she become a science libarian. She settled on nursing instead, and because she had skipped grades in school, she was a registered nurse and in Vietnam by the time she was twenty-one. She was one of the youngest nurses she knew.

She did two tours in Vietnam, from 1966 to 1968, working in an evacuation hospital as a surgical, intensive-care, or emergency-room nurse. An evac, as these hospitals were called, was the first place the wounded were brought from the field. Once they were stabilized, they were sent on to other military hospitals.

Nurses, it is often said, weren't in combat. It's true they didn't dodge bullets, but they could not avoid the bodies. "The first few times you cut someone's uniform off and the leg falls off, yes, your mind screams, but you stuff that down very, very quickly. You have to. If you lose control, they're going to die. It's as simple as that."

What kept her going then, and what helps a little now, is the knowledge that she was making a difference. She chose to spend a second year in Vietnam because "the wounded kept coming, the war was getting worse, and I was good at what I did." She knew that "these people would have a future because of all of the shit I was going through."

She was on her feet for seventy-two hours in an operating room during the Tet offensive in 1968. Her feet swelled so badly that she couldn't remove her boots for two days. But there was an incredible rush that came when someone they hadn't expected to make it through the night went home. Those are the ones she tries to think about when she opens her kitchen refrigerator and sees only gray and mangled arms and legs.

The horror and pain come from the memories of the ones who didn't make it. Some never regained consciousness and slipped from delirium into death. Some were angry, knowing they were too young to die. What did she say to them? "You tell them it sucks. Sometimes you don't say anything, you just hug them."

She never encouraged anyone to deny that he was dying. If a boy said, "I'm not going to make it, am I?," she would usually say, "It doesn't look good." There was a reason for that. She wanted the men to be able to say anything they needed to say before they died.

Intimacy was conveyed in words, silence, and touch. She was never afraid to touch her patients. "Rules don't apply. You're the nurse, the doctor, you're their parents, you're their girlfriend and their wife, you're the only thing they have, and whatever it takes, that's what you give. That's what you're there for. It was just automatic."

She wishes every soldier's mother could know how much her son was loved—by his buddies, by the medics, doctors, and nurses who cared for him. "Everything humanly possible that could have been done for every single one of them was done, and I don't think that any of them died alone and every one of them is missed."

David is one of the ones she remembers. Eighteen years later, she wrote a poem about his dying. One of his kidneys had been removed, and the other one was essentially destroyed and so was his liver. She knew, and he knew, that he would not make it through the night. He was conscious and coherent and they stayed together.

Hello, David—my name is Dusty.
I'm your night nurse.
I will stay with you.
I will check your vitals
*   every 15 minutes.*
I will document
*   inevitability.*
I will hang more blood
*   and give you something*
*   for your pain.*
I will stay with you
*   and I will touch your face.*

Yes, of course,
*   I will write your mother*
*   and tell her you were brave.*
I will write your mother
*   and tell her how much you loved her.*
I will write your mother
*   and tell her to give your bratty kid sister*
*   a big kiss and hug.*
What I will not tell her
*   is that you were wasted.*

I will stay with you
and I will hold your hand.
I will stay with you
and watch your life
flow through my fingers
into my soul.
I will stay with you
until you stay with me.

Goodbye, David—my name is Dusty.
I'm the last person
you will see.
I'm the last person
you will touch.
I'm the last person
who will love you.

So long, David—my name is Dusty.
David—who will give me something
for my pain?

There is another boy whose memory was important to her long after he died. She has forgotten his name, but not his face. "He was a little shrimp, probably weighed a hundred and twenty pounds. This kid saved my life. He wasn't even dirty. Not a mark on him. Probably had only been in Vietnam a few days. I don't know what the Army wanted with this kid, a little black kid who definitely should have been thrown back. I picked up his head to turn his head to check his pupils and his brains were running out his ear into my fingers. He had died from a concussive blast. I just looked at that brain tissue and thought, Whoever this was, he isn't here anymore. He had a mother who loved him and a future and a past and he came from somewhere. It's just such a fucking waste."

It was this memory that came back at a time when she was considering suicide. "I thought about pulling the trigger and splattering my brains all over the wall and I thought about this kid whose brains I had to wash off my hands and then I thought about whoever it might be that would have to come into my apartment and wipe the brains off the wall and wash my brains off their hands and I couldn't do that to someone."

A friend of hers who had been a medic did kill himself, and she was the one who found his body, on a morning they were supposed to go to the zoo.

• • •

Dusty went to Vietnam in 1966 because she hated the war. "If I went out into the streets, I would simply add one more body to the mob. It wouldn't do any good. The only way I knew how to stop killing and dying was to use the skill I was trained in. That's why I went."

When she came home, in 1968, she found that the hostility that greeted the soldiers was there for her, too. But there was an additional twist for women—the lewd comments from casual acquaintances and strangers. Sure, nurses were saviors on duty. Off duty they were sluts. Everyone, it seemed, knew that.

Those who protested the war at home felt Dusty was part of the war machine. Few bothered to find out how she felt: that she hated the war but had seen an utterly unparalleled fineness in so many of the men who fought there. She lost the energy to explain to those too stupid to understand.

The contributions of men who served in Vietnam were, by and large, scorned or ignored when they returned. But the contributions of women, specifically nurses, were simply unknown. The military, which prided itself on the records it kept in Vietnam—counting the number of enemy weapons captured, for example—cannot to this day say with certainty how many women served. The Army that sent them never bothered to count them. The estimate most frequently given is that a total of 7,500 women served in the military in Vietnam. Of these, 83.5 percent were nurses.

After two years in Vietnam, Dusty found it hard to readjust to nursing in the States. The intense professionalism and competence that were routine in Vietnam were lacking in much of what came after for Dusty. She tried emergency-room work, but it had none of the urgency of her experience in Vietnam.

She was floundering and she knew it. She found a man to take control of her life, and she married him. They tried to start a family, but she lost one child in a miscarriage and another, carried to full term, was born dead. Finally, as her marriage was breaking up, a son was born. He is now a sturdy teenager and the center of his mother's life.

She wanted more children but gave up the idea when a biopsy showed that dioxin, the chemical in Agent Orange, was present in her body fat. She is convinced that her pregnancy problems are related to her exposure to Agent Orange.

Years went by in which she didn't think about Vietnam or have nightmares or flashbacks. She was a single parent and working. It seemed she could keep herself together after all. She remarried. She was a survivor.

Then, in 1985, there were two anniversaries: the fortieth anniversary of the end of World War II and the tenth anniversary of the fall of Saigon. She was flooded with images of the two wars that had bracketed her life.

Her mother had survived the Holocaust. Dusty was an only child whose grandparents, aunts, uncles, and cousins died in the camps. It was not until she was thirty-six and joined a group of other children of Holocaust survivors that she began to understand how that experience had shaped her.

"There's no explanation, there's no marker, there's just a hole they fell into. It's very similar to what happened in my Vietnam experience. There are fifty-eight thousand men who just fell into a hole in eternity, and I saw it and no one wants to listen. People say, 'Oh, the Jews, they've always got problems. All we ever hear from the Jews is the Holocaust. Oh, the Vietnam veterans, the big crybabies, that's all they want to do is say how bad they've got it.' And all I want to do is punch their teeth down their throats."

Seeing the Vietnam War on television again in old news footage brought back nightmares. She had heard and read about the Vietnam Veterans Memorial and she knew she wanted to go there. She had a chance to go with her husband, and she did. It was a mistake. Unaware that he was married to a Vietnam vet, he treated the memorial as just another stop on the tourist trek through the capital. She cut the visit short, surprised at the vehemence of her reactions.

Back home she managed, at least on the outside, to keep a grip on her life. She went to work, came home, and made dinner. If nightmares wrecked her sleep, no one knew. And then it turned out that she was in Chicago at the time of one of the largest Vietnam veterans' parades ever held in the nation.

"I was totally unprepared for the emotions that hit me. I stood there all day watching the parade and the people. I don't think there were three seconds when tears were not rolling down my cheeks."

It became harder and harder to hide her past from her husband after that. He sensed something was wrong but had no idea what it could be. She said she couldn't explain it, but assured him it was not his fault. She wanted and needed to go back to the memorial, and two months later she did. "Somehow, it's as if all those faces just demand it once in a while. They just demand it. They say it's time to take forty-eight hours and think of us again."

She walked and she paced. She can look at anything on the west wall of the memorial, but when she is along the east wall, which includes her two years in Vietnam, she will not read the names, only the numbers at the base of the granite slabs. She doesn't want to discover anyone who left the evac hospital only to die somewhere else. She will not relinquish anyone from her column of triumphs.

She describes the visit as "profound and comforting." The memorial is the one place where she is comfortable about acknowledging her past. When she meets a vet and tells him she was a nurse, the reaction is always the same: " 'Son of a bitch! A nurse!' And then their next words are 'Thank you'—whether they were wounded or not, they always say it, and then they hug me or ask me if they can."

A few weeks after returning home she did what she hadn't done since Tet: she stayed up for three days and three nights, reliving and replaying her Vietnam memories. Her husband did not press her for an explanation and she did not offer one. She feared that if she confided in him, it would torpedo her marriage. He is older than she and once told her that he "never really noticed" the Vietnam War and that he thought anyone who voluntarily joined the Army had to be crazy. She also decided to find a therapist.

"I've tried to deny the past, I've tried to run away from it; that hasn't worked and I don't know what will work. Maybe nothing will. I'm just beginning to find out that I am not alone in the pain and I think that perhaps that will be the way out."

It is surprising, perhaps, to some people, but most who have served in Vietnam, despite the hideous aspects of their experience, do not regret that it happened and would go back. Dusty is no exception.

"I have been privileged to see, in absolutely the worst conditions that could exist, exactly how fine people can really be. To see the feeling these men had for their buddies and the things that they did and the caring they had, I think that's a rare privilege. I think I have been very honored by those circumstances."

She sips a diet Coke and thinks about what she would tell a nurse like herself who is in pain. "By going there, they did something that very few women do. If they can get through Vietnam, they can get through anything. When the nightmares wake them up in the middle of the night, or they open the closet door and they smell Vietnam, if they'll just put a face up there in their mind of someone that wouldn't be here if they hadn't gone, it gets a little better."

That's why she cried at the Chicago parade. Seeing vets with their children on their shoulders was the biggest thank-you she ever got. That's what she was fighting for: to resurrect some futures from the slaughter of war.

*He was the only young man from our town to die in the Vietnam
war. He was not the best boy the town produced, he was more like a
hoodlum most times. But he did not shirk his duty, nor did he take the
"easy" route to Canada. As a result, he made the ultimate sacrifice.
He may not have cared about his little home town, but in his way he
helped keep it free. There is no monument to record his sacrifice in
town, nor is his name read on Memorial Day. Some of us think of him
once in a while, though. Whenever I am home from my own service
with the army, I visit his gravesite.*

From all of us, "thanks."

For Captain Robert E. Mincey:

Dear "Pete,"

   Here's Guy's graduation picture. You would be so proud. *He's become a fine young man. He's very talented. Guy's written songs, beautiful ones, been in musical productions, draws, and paints.*

   I think I have done a pretty good job of raising him. I have taught him about you, our love, your love for him and your love and commitment to our country. In return, this love has been instilled in him and our values passed on. He's now in the Navy, going to electronics school and is at the top of his class. It was very hard to "let him go" and I pray for his safety.

   Thank you for your love and this child. I will always love you.

                                                                  Margaret

My son, John Dabonka

To My Lost Soldier

I see a soldier walking
And my heart skips a beat or two
As he nears, I hear him talking
Dear God! He sounds like you.

How tall and straight he stands, dear
Like you, so young in years
A lump comes in my throat, dear
And my eyes fill up with tears.

For I visioned it was you, dear
As you once walked by my side
And told me of your plans, dear
To one day take a bride.

But such was not to be, son
As your life for your country you gave
All that's left are memories, dear
As I stand here by your grave.

Virginia Dabonka
Weehawken, New Jersey

I don't feel guilty because you died and I live. I feel guilty because I have failed you. You died to provide me an opportunity to accomplish something. Not only have I not done anything with my life, my lack of accomplishment is the result of the worst of all sins, lack of discipline, irresponsibility, lack of courage to try.

I may sound ironic to the living, but hopefully, not to you. I need you again, your support, spirit and prayers. Please help me help myself to learn the dedication I lack and need to accomplish something that will make worthwhile your sacrifice.

I think I feel guilty when I think about you. I felt the war was justified and went to college with a school deferment. I don't know how any of you felt about the war; I do know you fought and died. Not even the lottery required me to exert any courage for my convictions, my number was 333.

I don't wish that I fought and died. Rather I wish for an opportunity to put myself on the line, to put my courage up for my convictions. Hopefully, it will make up for my lack of guts the last time around.

Excerpts from a journal left at
the Vietnam Veterans Memorial
by Michael Massaro

———•———

I VOLUNTEERED for the Army on 1 March, 1968, at Camden Post Office. I left Camden on a Trailways bus for Newark, N.J., where I was to be sworn in. After being sworn in, we were on another bus for Ft. Dix. After my 18th birthday, my orders came for Vietnam.

I arrived in Vietnam on 5 March, 1969, Saigon, Ton Son Nhut Airbase, on a commercial plane, stewardess American girls, and the last American girls I would see for 17 months. When I got off the plane, the first thing I felt was the heat and I could smell the shit burning. That's what everybody said when they came back from Nam to the 82nd Airborne back at Ft. Bragg, N.C., coming into Vietnam you knew it was Nam even though you've never seen Vietnam before; from the plane you could see smoke coming out of the mountains. The mountains were dark green and black, except where bombs had hit. You could see patches of orange clay all over the mountains. You could feel fear building in the plane, some of the orange bomb craters had water in them, they almost looked like sand quarries, like the quarries we swam in back home. It was a strange war, I could see already.

My orders now were for Company D, the men call it Dog Company. We would go on patrols from the rear, into the mountains around An Khe, I saw my first montagnard in the mountains of An Khe. We used them to show us the way through the mountains, they knew where the booby traps and land mines could be found. They carried cross bows as weapons, excellent point men. On one patrol we were on with the montagnard people we were way up in the mountains, for miles on the trail we were on there were pungi sticks on both sides of us. All the trees were standing, but all the life was gone, not one speck of green or brown, just gray. We had about twenty men, four half tracks, a few choppers, two men got wounded when a sniper opened up on us coming up the trail. When he shot at us, the men dove into the pungi sticks, almost through their bodies. The Viet Cong were known for dipping the pungi sticks in human shit or poison to cause infection or death. After two weeks, Company D was to move out to Quin Nhon, North Highway One. We always moved north, the whole 17 months I was there, never south back to some kind of civilization.

We were right in the middle of everything, to our front the gasoline and oil tanks, and Quin Nhon city and ports, R & R center, Highway One, the Viet Cong wanted this point where we sat, they could wipe out Quin Nhon from here, to our rear was a leper colony, both sides mountains, but it was a peaceful place, beautiful, you could see the South China Sea, the sun would sparkle off it. To pass time we would clean out each other's boils with Q-tips, just spin the Q-tips around inside the boil until it was cleaned out of pus, this would go on every day throughout the year in Vietnam, boils and more boils, my chest is full of blackheads from boils. After a few weeks, the vacation was over. We were now moving to Bong Son, again north on Highway One, a few miles south of Hue.

I took a plane to An Khe, a few hundred miles north of Saigon. We had one week of jungle training and then after jungle training we reported to our company, Co E, 4/503, 173rd Airborne. Most of the men were out in the mountains and jungles. We were told to grab a cot for the night. Tomorrow we would be going to our platoons, in all different areas. It was strange, nobody was around to tell you anything. We put our gear on a cot and took off to see what we could find to do all night. There was a beer hall in the back outside, they showed movies. What luck we thought. We sat on the ground. As soon as the movie came on a sniper started shooting at the movie area. He hit two men, one killed on the spot, the other wounded in the head. The gook sniped until the gun ships came and blew the mountain away. About an hour later, the movie came back on, the gook came out again and started shooting again. The movie was cancelled. We went back to our gear and cots. I don't think any of us slept. I laid there all night and thought "I'm never going to make it home. I'll never survive." You could hear the guns going off in the distance, then guns returning fire. Why didn't I stay in school? Back in Blackwood, I missed Highland High School. Now, what I wouldn't have given to be back there, stepfather and everything. Nothing was like Vietnam, then and now.

It was a few days after Easter Sunday when we moved from Quin Nhon to Bong Son. We got on choppers again. It was a long ride.

The choppers landed at the new home of the 173rd Airborne, LZ North English. We, Company D, were to go to a village, Tam Quam, off the South China Sea. We were to sweep from the village of Tam Quam which was about two or three miles to Highway One, pushing all the Viet Cong or North Vietnamese to the other half of our unit waiting in ambush.

The first twenty men moved out of the clearing and into the village. The earth turned upside down, blood and skin were flying through the air, pieces of flesh and blood were hitting me in the face, hot blood, I could feel it burning my face. Men were laying all over the place, crying and dead. Some of the bodies didn't even look like people, it looked like the trash outside a meat store, and the smell of burning flesh, I can still smell it when it rains, I can smell that smell.

Sgt. Cook, Joe Longoria were killed on the spot. Sixteen others were either dead or in pieces. We got the wounded out of the village and layed them in the rice paddies arms and legs off, stomach out on the ground. I remember laying next to Clapfulder, I picked his belly up off the ground and put it back inside his body. He said, "Thanks Mike for being here with me, please don't leave me here alone, do you have a joint rolled?" Sgt. E-7, I don't remember his name, was on the other side of me, the side of his head was gone and he was smoking a cigarette, another guy's foot was off.

When the choppers left there were only six men left that would stay until morning when the choppers would come back for us. Me and my forward observer were calling in illumination rounds, to light up the area until we could get out which wasn't until daylight. All night I thought about putting my friends in body bags, picking up pieces of their bodies, a boot with a leg, no body, arms, feet, heads, the night went on forever. I've never been the same since. The smell of that night never left me, the sight never left either.

Morning came, the chopper came to pick us up. When we got to the rear, we got clean clothes and a bath, hot food if you wanted it, nobody ate, nobody said a word, and the people from the rear acted like nothing had happened to us.

A few hours later, we went back to the village of Tam Quam. When we got to the center of the village, the Sgt. in charge had us remove the bullets from our weapons. We all thought they were crazy, we just lost half our platoon here, now the Army wants the Vietnamese to see we are friendly. A few men were told they would be court-martialed if they didn't follow the order to take the bullets out of their weapons. It was crazy.

• • •

I was now in Vietnam about six months. My time came for a two-week R & R to Thailand. While in the rear my first night, a Sgt. told me that one of my grandparents had died and that my other grandparent was about to die. I cancelled my R & R for the next day so I could call home.

I couldn't get a call through so they sent me back to my company at LZ English, but in a day or two I was on my way to R & R in Thailand so I could try again. While I was standing there, a lieutenant walked by. "You, soldier, they need a man, an RTO, out at A Company. Get your gear and report to the LZ for a chopper back to the mountains." I tried to tell him what was happening. He said "I don't want to hear your shit, soldier." I said "Go Fuck Yourself," and then went and got my gear. The Captain of Company E said "I am writing you up for an Article 15, for disrespect to an officer and for disobeying an order." I said "I was disrespectful, but I was on my way back to the LZ for a chopper."

About three weeks after my court martial, I was brought to the stockade in Saigon, Long Binh jail.

For two months, I sat in the stockade in Vietnam, in an iron connex box, 6x6, the boxes sat in the sun, you couldn't move around at all. At night when the Viet Cong were rocketing the city, I just sat praying the rockets wouldn't fall inside the compound. We didn't get out of the boxes for anything, not showers, not even to go to the bathroom. I was gassed, beaten, pissed on, kicked, not fed for a few days, no water some days, bread and water for three days at a time, I was in the connex box about two or three weeks, cuffed to the bottom of the box, the heat got so bad and the smell; I would try to choke myself to death, but I would only get dizzy. I had malaria while in the connex box. I would get chills and sweat, but nobody cared in there. I think they wanted us to die, then we would never get to talk about this hell hole. After two months of Long Binh jail, I and a hundred others were shipped to Okinawa. Someone was coming to see the stockade in Vietnam so they were getting us out of there.

It sounds crazy, but after the stockade and the rear, Vietnam doesn't seem that bad. You knew out there who was trying to kill or cause you harm, you could defend yourself, out there they didn't have rights. In the rear we were the people without rights, and they let you know every day that you don't have any rights when you're a soldier. It's strange that most of the men I met volunteered for

Vietnam to uphold people's rights, when you get to Vietnam you find out everybody has rights except for the soldier out in the mountains, jungle, rice paddies fighting the war, the only rights you have are to die.

Sometimes we would see Vietnamese fishing, we would help by throwing a grenade in the water. All the fish would rise to the top of the water, dead. The man fishing would go crazy, like he never seen that many fish before at one time, he was there for hours, us, five minutes. They looked at us like we were gods or something, sometimes I think they got mad because all the man did was fish, we left him with nothing to do except lay out booby traps. I had so much fish and rice in Vietnam to eat that now it's like I had it yesterday. I'm still sick of fish and rice and chicken.

It was night on LZ Graham about mid-June '70. I was asleep on the top of our bunker an hour after I finished my four-hour guard or whatever when I heard Sgt. Van calling, "Mike, the Viet Cong are coming through the wire." Just then I heard a claymore go off, one of our bunkers went up in flames. I saw one gook pushing at something at the Command bunker window. He had a grenade in one hand and was pushing at the board. I shot once with my M-16. I hit him in the chest, he bent over for a second, then started pushing at the window again. I could see the blood coming from his chest, he didn't have any clothes on, I shot again, this time he went back and over. He was dead, I still see his eyes in my sleep, the red and black of that night, like it was yesterday. A few minutes later I saw another gook come and pick the dead gook up, he started running. I shot again and again. We found three dead Viet Cong. They had what looked like G-strings on and that was it; black stuff on their skin for camouflage.

Getting back to the patrol with the lieutenant, we got the gooks out of the tunnel, both dead, we started back to the wounded gook, he was on his belly trying to crawl back to the village, we caught him coming out, me and Moore wanted to bring him back alive, he was just like us, about twelve years old, black pajamas, Ho Chi Minh sandals, a bamboo pipe, a bag of good grass. We stood over him wanting to give him help, the lieutenant pushed me and Moore out of the way and put sixteen rounds in his back. I just walked away with Moore, our hands leaning on each other, crying.

I didn't feel like I belonged. The other people that didn't go, the people that protested and burned the flag in Washington, hated me because I went and fought, I was a man without friends, nobody to help me, no one to listen, no one to tell. Fear drove me inside myself. And now, today, about twelve years later, I'm in the same situation today, except for my wife and a few friends and twelve Vietnam vets I have someone to talk to, and maybe, just maybe, I can come home. I've been a P.O.W. in my own mind for twelve long years, flashbacks every day, sometimes a few in one day. A few days after I was home, my family gave me a homecoming party, some friends and family. I remember it was raining so we all sat under the car port. Rain always does something to my head. I could even smell Vietnam, even though I was home for a few days, the people packed under the car port all together gives you the feeling of Vietnam, close net feeling.

Nobody wanted to hear Vietnam. My mother watched it on TV every night, my older brother Jim was in Vietnam in the Marine Corps for two years on the DMZ. My mother had enough of the war, we all had enough of the war, but for me, the war isn't over yet. My wife's war isn't over yet either. When will it be over, when can I turn the light out at the end of the tunnel? I hope the light at the end of the tunnel isn't the sun.

ROGER A. DIXON

Private First Class, Company B, 3rd Battalion,
22nd Infantry Regiment, 25th Infantry Division
NOVEMBER 27, 1948–JANUARY 17, 1969

Dear Roger,

Though many years have gone by, and you are in another home, every day I miss you and long to see your young face. You are always tucked away in a special corner of my heart. There is never a day I do not think of you and why you had to die, but I know you are in a safe place way beyond the sky. Your Dad has just gone and things are not the same, but I try to carry on just the same. You were a special boy to me and you will always be locked in my heart and my memories. The years have come and gone and I miss you more as time goes on.

All my love,
Mom

———•———

I don't guess it will be too much longer until I will be a father. It is kind of hard for me to believe, but also, I can hardly wait until next month. I hope all of you are fine and don't worry about me.

IT WAS his last letter home; twenty-four hours later, Roger Dixon was dead, killed by "friendly fire"—the military's gruesome phrase for the accidental killing of Americans by other Americans in Vietnam. Roger Dixon's child was born three days after he died.

The letter is translucent with age and on the verge of disintegration. Roger's mother, Polly Dixon, has kept it in her wallet for seventeen years, referring to it often, as she does this late December day at a restaurant in Richmond, Virginia. "I've been better this week, but last week, I don't think there was a day gone by that I didn't shed some tears," she says. "Roger loved Christmas. Couple of mornings I was sitting at the kitchen table drinking my coffee and the tears were streaming down my face, thinking about him."

The holidays are difficult for Polly. Roger's birthday comes on or near Thanksgiving, and he was scheduled to come home for Christmas in 1969. Yet when you sit in her immaculate brick house, you see Christmas everywhere. There are garlands of plastic pine and thick red-and-white candles on the mantel with a collection of ornamental music boxes. She has had the same artificial tree for eighteen years, and it is decorated with ornaments she has made herself over the last four decades.

Polly can't help but mourn another Christmas without her son. "You can put it behind you enough that you can deal with life," she says, "but I cannot put that boy aside like he never existed. I'm not even going to try."

Roger was her second son to serve in Vietnam. His older brother, James, was in the Air Force, but his tour did not make Polly feel uneasy. "I knew it was dangerous, but I never had the feeling about him that we all had about Roger.

"It was just after he left for Vietnam," she remembers. "I was cleaning the backyard, and I guess I had Roger on my mind. Well, just in that instant, a vision of him dropped down in front of me and he was in a coffin. About two weeks later, I was cleaning the bedroom, and the same thing happened. I stood at the foot of the bed and a vision came down in front of my eyes and he was in a coffin. That Sunday, when I went to church, I sat there and the tears just streamed down my face the whole time."

Roger himself had not been fatalistic about going to Vietnam. But the night before he left he told his dad, "I'm not afraid of what I'm going to do, because I took in my training well. I'm just afraid of what somebody else's mistake is going to do."

According to a boyhood pal of Roger's who was stationed nearby in Vietnam, Roger's platoon had been on a night patrol in Tay Ninh province when they detonated some Claymore mines set out by their own point man. The platoon leader, who was brand-new, had failed to check with the point man on the location of the mines before leading his men out into the jungle. Roger, who was the radioman, and four others, including the platoon leader, were killed. Roger Dixon had been in Vietnam for thirty-seven days.

The Army, in a letter to Roger's widow, acknowledged that the death was accidental but had a different account of the tragedy: "At approximately 11:45 P.M., Roger's platoon was mistaken for a hostile force by another platoon and a firefight ensued."

Polly Dixon believes Roger's buddy's account. But she doesn't blame her son's comrades. "We were told that Roger's platoon leader was new and it was the first time out," she says. "He made an error, what can you do? How can you condemn another twenty-year-old boy? It doesn't bring any of the five back."

Her anger, which has been slowly abating these past seventeen years, has been reserved for America's leaders. "It took eight days for Roger's body to get back. . . . I walked the floor for eight nights. You're angry at the government, you're angry at the president, but I was never angry at God.

"When I went to that funeral parlor, they had the glass over him," she want on. "Every time I looked at him, I could hear him say, 'Mama, please don't cry.' But when they got ready to close the coffin, and we were going to look at him for the last time, I yelled out, 'Roger, my baby!' I wasn't aware that I did it, but they told me later. The tears finally came."

Roger was the youngest of her three children. She remembers her doctor telling her in the delivery room on a cold November day in 1948, "You can give him to me; he is the prettiest thing I ever did see." Some of his baby pictures are in the den and he looks like a child who blew ashore in a gale of laughter. An eight-point buck he killed when he was sixteen gazes over the photos with a frozen stare.

"Roger was a boy that didn't like to be still," Polly reminisces. "He was constantly on the move. He liked to be active and outdoors. He did read, but the only thing he read was the *Reader's Digest* and the Bible."

He considered college, but the main thing on his mind when he graduated from high school was work. He wanted to save money and secure a future that way. His parents, worried about the draft, suggested he enlist in the Air Force or Navy. He told Polly, "Mama, I just can't stand the thought of being away from home for four years. I'll take my chances."

When he was nineteen, shortly after he married a young woman he had dated throughout high school, his draft number came up and Roger, who had never been away from Richmond, went off to basic training. He had one brief visit home before leaving for Southeast Asia.

Polly always wanted to see the Vietnam Veterans Memorial, but she wasn't able to make the short trip from Richmond until four years after it was dedicated. Arthritis has made walking difficult, and when she finally went, she did so in a wheelchair. A group of veterans from Richmond took turns pushing her wheelchair around the site, wrapping a blanket around her when it got too cold.

When she finally saw Panel 34 West with Roger's name on it, Polly found some solace for her pain. "I don't think you can help but feel a closeness, that maybe there's a part of him there. That was the reason for writing the letter; it's stupid, because I know he couldn't read it, but to me, he could understand what I was saying. It is a communication with him, to him; I can communicate with him though I can't touch him or hug him or kiss him."

Polly keeps his last letter tucked inside its tattered envelope in her wallet; it is the last part of him she has that she can touch. The letter says nothing profound. Roger did not meditate on war or sense that dying was all that he had left to do. It was a letter home to Mom from a boy who had never been away from home until he was drafted into the Army.

Mom, I got your package yesterday. I can always use something to eat because all the guys in the platoon help me with the eating. How are you and everyone else doing? We came out into base camp the day before yesterday. They are giving me a few days rest before we go back out in the field. I hate to go back out there and I wasn't out there half as long as the other guys were. And I am pretty sure we are going back out there tomorrow morning . . .

My Lover Died in Action

Away across the sea
Lies the man that I love,
He was fighting for our country
When God called him from above.

We were living for our love
Never knowing that the day
When he was called to fight
That it would end this way.

When the telegram came
My heart sank with fear
And as I read it over
My eyes filled with tears.

My darling now is sleeping
While God watches from above,
And I sit alone weeping
At the loss of the one I love.

James—

Sorry they wouldn't keep it down longer so I could get you, brother. I wish it was me instead of you. Just wanted you to know I love ya, brother. Still talk to Cathy and your babies. They're grown and proud of you. You're me and I'm you. I'll always watch over them for you, brother. God Bless. I'll see ya soon, James. Just thought I would let you know everything's okay.

The Doc

My dearest Paul,

I finally got here—a beautiful monument for you. I miss you, and I know you're watching over me. I love you,

Your wife

JAMES ROBERT KALSU

First Lieutenant, C Battery, 2nd Battalion, 11th Artillery,
101st Airborne Division (Airmobile)
APRIL 13, 1945–JULY 21, 1970

My prayer, my dear and sweet husband, is that the world would forever know peace so that never again will death separate and permanently sear the hearts of families torn by the tragedies of war. I await the day when the Lord reunites us in heaven. Honey, I love you forever.

Your wife, Jan

Daddy,

How I long for the day we will be together again. So many times have I wanted for you to put your arm around me, wipe a tear from my eye, or just to laugh and tease with me. I think if we could be together we would be really close. I'm proud of you and the values you stood for. I love you, Jill

Dad,

How I've missed the father and son things we could have done, the knowledge and love you could have given me. I can't wait for the time we are reunited to share our love and talk to each other. You are truly a person I can look up to.

I love you, Bob

———————•———————

ONE NIGHT long ago, when she was in boarding school, Jan Darrow awakened her roommates. "I just had this terrible dream," the fifteen-year-old girl told her friends. "A woman gave birth to a little son and she couldn't tell her husband because he died before the baby was born."

Years later, in a hospital room in Oklahoma City, the nightmare came true. It was the day after the birth of her son. "Dr. McGuire, the obstetrician, stayed at the head of my bed and he cupped me in his arms," Jan remembers. "And this poor soldier came in and, God love him, he was crying after he found out I had just had a child, but he had his orders and he said, 'I'm sorry to inform you but your husband has been killed.' I just told Dr. McGuire, 'I want to go home, I'm not going to stay here.' The nurses all were crying."

Bob Kalsu was running to meet a chopper that had just landed at firebase Ripcord, on a desolate jungle mountaintop, when he was killed. It happened on his wife's due date, July 21, 1970, and Jan is sure he was hoping that the helicopter might bring news of his baby. "He never got to know about Bobby," she says. "We made a tape of the delivery and they sent the Red Cross up there to tell him, but it got there a day or two after he died."

Afterward, Jan Kalsu moved back to her parents' house with her twenty-month-old daughter, Jill, and her newborn son. At age twenty-two, she was the widow of the only pro-football player to die in the Vietnam War.

Bob Kalsu had just finished his first season as an offensive guard with the Buffalo Bills when he suited up as a first lieutenant. The Bills had named him their rookie of the year in 1969, and he had just become a father. He and Jan seemed to be starring in the all-American fairy tale: football star marries college sweetheart and, surrounded by their beautiful children, they live happily ever after.

Bob and Jan were devout Catholics, and the church was the fulcrum of their lives. Jan remembers that shortly after Bob got his orders for Vietnam, she was kneeling at the altar and said, "Lord, if you feel you need Bob more than I do, at least give us a son." When she found out she was pregnant just before Bob departed for Southeast Asia, she told him about her prayer. "He said, 'Oh, Jan, God is not going to do that, he's going to bring me back home.' "

But there was a summer funeral instead of a Christmas homecoming. "I was so devastated over my husband, there were times I couldn't even cope," she says. "Sometimes I just couldn't take one more minute. I'd just throw myself across the bed and start crying; little Bobby would be in the infant seat in the family room and Jill would go and get the Kleenex by the bed and hand it to me. 'Here, Mommy, I take care of baby.' And honest to God, she'd sit right by him and watch him. She'd even close the bedroom door, and after ten minutes, I'd get my composure, get my act together, and brace myself."

Her faith in God sustained her then and still does. But it has never precluded anger. "I went through a bitter time—oh, nothing makes you angrier than when people come to you and say things like 'It will be okay, things will get better, honey, you're young, you'll get married again soon.' " Words like that, though well-intentioned, were not comforting.

True comfort and support came from her husband's parents, Leah and Frank Kalsu, who also lived in Oklahoma City. Bob was their only child, and like survivors who stumble out of the same smoky, mangled wreckage, they banded together with Jan to help her raise her children. "We did so much crying and hugging and leaning onto each other," Jan recalls. "We were always sharing it, keeping it open." Over the years, the sharing of their grief and love has strengthened them all.

Bob Kalsu was a natural athlete. Football came easily to him and he played it throughout high school and college, but his favorite sport was golf. He was more competitive than aggressive; Jan Kalsu remembers that when her husband had a bad day and needed to blow off steam, he'd come home and reach for the Chinese checkers.

They met in college, when Bob was a junior, an offensive guard at the University of Oklahoma, and Jan was a freshman at Central State; a mutual friend fixed them up a blind date. Hearing she'd be meeting someone named Bob Kalsu, Jan asked, "But is he Chinese?" (The name is actually Czech.)

Love flourished. Jan told her sister after her first date that she had met the man she wanted to marry. And within several months Bob was as committed as she; they began to plan a future. He wanted to play professional football, and then teach and coach. She wanted five or six children, maybe more. The wedding took place in January 1968, just after Bob played his final collegiate game in the Orange Bowl.

Both the Dallas Cowboys and the Denver Broncos were pursuing him, but some professional teams seemed worried about the implications of Bob's ROTC background—no one wanted to invest in a player who might be marched off to war. But when Bob and Jan returned from their honeymoon, they found out he had been drafted by the Buffalo Bills. The Bills wanted a beefier Bob, and he added 35 pounds to his already hefty 225-pound frame; when Jan learned she was pregnant, the couple joked about getting big together.

Jill was born in November 1968. "She was the delight of her father," Jan recalls. "He'd get insulted if anyone said she looked like me! In church, it looked like he was carrying a football when he was carrying her down the aisle." But before Jill was a year old, Bob Kalsu was on his way to Vietnam, the jersey with number 51 on it stashed away. "I can still remember the day he got the orders," says Jan. "He just cried."

Bob's mother, Leah Kalsu, wrote to Carl Albert, the Oklahoma congressman who was then majority leader; she asked if there was any way her son could avoid going to Vietnam. Albert replied optimistically. But Bob Kalsu wasn't looking for favors. His mother summed up his attitude this way: "Why should anyone be exempt from going? You always have to take the bad with the good."

In the spring of 1970, the Kalsus spent their last time together, in Hawaii. Bob had already seen six months of heavy combat in Vietnam, and the Army flew him to Honolulu for some R and R. Jan was already seven months pregnant, and Jill was not quite a year and a half when they traveled to meet Bob. Before their husbands arrived, the waiting wives were briefed by the military. "They took us into this room and told us, 'Don't discuss any kind of family problems; don't tell them anything that would upset them. These men have been through hell,' " says Jan.

A short while later, she and Bob were reunited. "He was totally exhausted," Jan remembers. "He just wanted to sleep. But for some reason, our hotel had fireworks. He thought he was in the combat zone and I saw this grown man tear out for cover.

"I would try to ask him what it was like and he would say, 'Oh, Jan, if you could see the people there, little babies walking those roads naked'—and that's as far as he would let me into that part of his life."

A home movie tells the rest of the story. A young family is on a lush beach. Jan is very pregnant and sits on a blanket. Daddy and daughter play in the shallow surf. They splash and wave to Mommy. Jill runs to the edge of the water, then back to the blanket with her father, a tall, strong, and gentle man. It is a simple and tender scene but brutally sad because everyone watching it today knows how this story is going to end.

"When he had to go back, the Army put us on a tram kind of thing to take us away from the plane," Jan says. "He didn't want to leave us and he held my hand until the movement of the tram pulled us away. I said, 'Bob, be careful,' He choked up, cried, and told me to be careful, too, that I was going to give birth to our baby—that was the last thing he said."

These days, both Jill and Bob Kalsu, Jr., are honor students at a parochial high school in Oklahoma City. It is still difficult for them to talk about their father without crying.

"When I was younger," Jill begins, "I dreamed about him, but now I really just *think* about him and how my life would be different if he were with me." Though she studied the Vietnam War in the eighth grade, Jill blanked most of it out. She may want to know more about it later, but not now. "I don't want to know what my dad went through."

As for her younger brother, the first thing you notice about Bob Kalsu, Jr., is that he's tall, well built, and athletic, just like his namesake. Bob junior has a smile that seems shy, mischievous, and sincere all at once. A few years ago, he put his feelings about losing his father into a poem:

Why God

Why did you do it
Why did he die
You didn't even give him time
To tell his own son "hi"

Why is there war
What does it show
Why us Lord
Why did he go

Why him Lord
He was such a good Christian
Why was it him
That you gave such a short mission

Why my father God
What did he ever do
You didn't even give him time
To tell his own son "I love you"

There are so many others
Why did it have to be him
Why did he leave
Why wasn't it them

The love he showed for others
Could have been for me too

Why him God
Was he just for you

It hurts many others
Not just me
I guess I'll never understand
I guess I'll never see

Why my father God
What did he ever do
You didn't even give him time
To tell his own son "I love you."

Several years after he wrote that, Bob junior's mother was going through a safe-deposit box and found a cassette tape her husband sent home from Vietnam just before he was killed. Jan played the tape for her children, who heard their father talk to his wife, speak lovingly to Jill, then finish his recorded message with these words to his unborn child: "And now for you, Baby K, Daddy loves you and pretty soon I'll be home to hold you." Fifteen years after his father died, Bobby Kalsu heard the words meant just for him. He took the tape into his bedroom and played it over and over for a week.

Jan Kalsu recently decided to do something she was sure she would never do: marry again. She rarely dated, and when Bob Mc-Laughlin, a medical management consultant, came into her life, she did everything in her power to push him away. But his gentle persistence and patient love finally won her over. "Bob doesn't threaten my former life; in fact, he has worked me through a lot of healing," she says. It was his idea to visit the Vietnam Veterans Memorial. He had taken a business trip to New York with his own children by an earlier marriage as well as Jill and Bob junior. When he arrived in Manhattan he called Jan on impulse and suggested she come East and that they visit Washington. She cried. She'd always hoped to see the memorial but never thought she could afford to go.

Jan quickly packed, and included pictures of her children; she would leave them at the wall. "I wanted him to be able to see what his children looked like and what a blessing they are," she says. The night before they went to the memorial, Jan, Jill, and Bob junior wrote the messages on the backs of the snapshots. When they got to the memorial, the sensation was eerie.

"I felt like I wanted to tiptoe because I was with all of these men's spirits," Jan says. "Although I knew Bob's body was buried here at home, I felt like he was there." Jan and her fiancé cried there together.

Vietnam means only sadness to the Kalsu family. Jan finds no meaning in the war that subverted her future. Though in the years following Bob's death, she felt guilty about her anger—it seemed almost un-American to her—she now feels that "a lot of upper men in the government have a lot to answer for. . . . As far as I'm concerned, they let a lot of our men get murdered. It was like they put them out there and said, 'See if you can make it.' "

The Army abandoned firebase Ripcord two days after Bob Kalsu died defending it. Like Jan, Bob's mother, Leah, feels some disillusionment and bitterness about her government. "My son didn't die for his country but because of it." But that will never matter as much as losing her only child. "You don't ever get over it," she says. "You just learn to live with it a little better. If you don't, you die." After thinking quietly for a moment she adds, "A shattered heart can be glued together again and still look like a heart that will pass as a heart —but it's not the same."

Insertion

Anxiety mounts up
The time is near

No hot LZ
Is causing this fear.

Numerous thoughts crowd,
How will I feel?

Approaching the wall
Scared. How will I deal?

The names are my
Comrades, Friends and peers

For a long lost time
I have held my tears.

Tom McCarthy
69–70
Americal D Troop 1/1 Cav

Hi Son:

Once again I am here at "The Wall" to visit you. Of course it is the guys from Massachusetts who brought me here.

Your twin is OK. Your 3 sisters and I take care of him for you. He skipped his birthday in May, as usual, but in our hearts we all observed it.

Dad is up there with you now so take care of each other till we all meet. You know I think of you every day and Terry, every time I look at Jerry I see you.

I love you son.

God Bless you and take care of you for me.

Love,
Mom

JOHN THOMAS HOLTON, JR.

First Lieutenant, Company A, 1st Battalion, 501st Infantry,
101st Airborne Division
MARCH 29, 1948–JULY 7, 1968

Dear Lieutenant,

 It's autumn now. Glorious colors decorate the Piedmont of North Carolina. I hope somehow that you can appreciate all this. Maybe, wherever you are, it is more glorious and colorful. No way I can know. Where do warriors go? Especially cherub warriors like we were. Hell if I know, Lieutenant. I suppose many people think warriors naturally go to hell. Or is that just generals? I don't know, Lieutenant. It has been a helluva a long time. Eighteen years.

 I tried to contact your folks once. I failed miserably. Not that I know what to say particularly. I can only imagine their pain. I do recall seeing your father once at Ft. Campbell in December of '67. Shit, we were just kids then, both of us. You were a Lieutenant and I a lowly E-1. Thanks for caring, John. We suffered enough together.

 I'm a writer now, along with being an insurance man, father and several other things some less than friendly people call me. I don't know exactly what you are now. Hell, I'm nearly 38. Nam was half my life ago. Only thing I've seen about you since '68 is your name on the killed in action list in the 101st yearbook, your name on this great black stone in Washington. That's it, man. Remember that company picture we had made at Campbell? I gave it to Gary Scott's mother in 1983. I wrote a poem about you which I consider one of my best and I've written about our time together in Alpha Company.

 You know Lt., when I returned from Hawaii R & R in July of 1968 and came busting into the XO tent at Sally carrying a couple of bottles of rum you had paid for, never in my life have I faced such trauma as when Dan Brentel told me you got blown away. Freaked me bad, Lieutenant, beaucoup.

 Similar thing happened in '69 when I returned from R & R in Hong Kong. Captain John Gay gave me money to buy jump boots for him at a special Kowloon cobbler. I returned with whore stories to tell, boots in hand, only to find that Captain Gay had been blown away and might never be able to walk in those boots. Jesus. Deja Vu.

 Remember Michael? He extended his tour. Stayed on the line six months, supposedly a hero. You know he was a helluva fighter. The asshole. Remember the time in February of '68 after Tet when he *dangled those baby chicks over the fire to watch them dance? He was a sadistic asshole. Guess what? I'm home from Nam a year or so and there is this national news report about a Nam vet who dressed up in his fatigues and M-16 and went out robbing gas stations. No shit. Hero Nam warrior a poor victim? My ass, a few months later he was on the Dick Cavett show. What a dildo!*

Guess I better wind this shit down, Lieutenant. If I go on too much, some people in the world might get the idea that my brain damage is even greater. Fuck 'em sir. Hell, you and I went through too much. Remember the drowning episode in January, 1968? How about Tet and all that fucking night humping up near Hai Lang, the mountains, An Lo, and of course March 16 and the dead monks. Hell, I recall vividly eating dinner with you in that blown out pagoda just a few minutes before I got wounded June 10, 1968. We faced it, eh, Lieutenant? Guess I better sign off—I did write you a poem, man.

John Holton

Holton was from Jacksonville
Amigos he and I
Gave me cash to buy some booze
Waved to me goodbye.

I went to Hawaii
To spend my R & R,
Rest up from the fighting,
Nurse my battle scars.

I strolled on beaches in paradise
Civilization I would tap.
Holton humped the boonies
Tripped a booby trap.

Back came I to battle
Toting Holton's rum
I cried when I discovered
He was blown to kingdom come.

Sat inside a bunker
Stared into the dark
Saw John Holton's image
A friend had made his mark.

> *Your RTO, rum-drinking buddy,*
> *Woodall*

———————•———————

PHIL WOODALL AND JOHN HOLTON were together when they stumbled on a group of slaughtered monks. In the peculiar and predictable context of war, they never talked about it, but it was an image that haunted Phil Woodall for years to come. He remembers March 16, 1968, for what happened to the monks of Phu Vang; the rest of the world remembers the date for what happened a hundred miles south of there in a town called My Lai.

John Holton was Phil Woodall's lieutenant. He had led the men of Company A through an all-day battle, which had begun before breakfast when their platoon was ambushed in a nameless village. The fighting was terrible; one of their sergeants was killed, several men were badly wounded, and the chopper that came in to rescue them was shot down. When it was finally over, Holton and Phil Woodall, his radioman, were walking away, down a path. They had just crossed an irrigation trench when they found the monks. "There was a yard full of them, out in front of this little monastery," Woodall remembers. "Holton and I, we saw this for maybe a twenty-second glimpse—and it has never gone away. Who killed them, the white-robed monks, covered in blood?" Woodall thinks the monks might have been mowed down by gunships. Or perhaps they were caught in the downpour of artillery that saturated the area during the battle. "Maybe," he says, "it is the not knowing that is so bad about this." After eighteen years, he wrote a poem about that awful day:

> *. . . We are*
> *The sons of My Lai*
> *Hardly, deadly*
> *Anymore.*

Aged, crusty,
Crippled
Limping
Toward midnight.

Stalked
By blackness,
Wave so long
Warrior

Say farewell
To the
Monks
Of Phu Vang

Or
Bid goodbye
To
Breathing

How can
I forget
A Buddhist
Bloodbath day?

March
Sixteenth
In nineteen
Sixty-eight.

Their death—
Too many—
Not the least
Insane.

Phil Woodall got to Vietnam just before the start of the Tet offensive in 1968. As the new kid in the combat zone, he was the "cherry." Once, on Phil's first time out, the platoon was wading across a river and he and Holton were slightly ahead of the rest. Suddenly, the river bottom disappeared. Weighted down by all the excess gear that newcomers think they need, Phil Woodall started to sink. He remembers staring at the sun from beneath the water's surface. "I thought I was a goner, but I could see the light," he remembers. "I got real calm, which was a big shock. It was so peaceful, it was unbelievable." Holton and some other soldiers saved him from drowning.

That night the platoon slept in the bush, and it changed Phil. He was terrified in the dark and was covered with ants; he was still wet and insects seemed to find every inch of him. "From that time on, I wasn't so naïve or gung ho," he says. "Dying seemed real. I was very lonely, very cold, very scared. What in hell am I doing here? It was one of the longest nights of my life, a frightful night, hard to forget or remember."

One of the few things that made Vietnam at all tolerable for Phil Woodall was John Holton, a patriotic Florida Baptist who once wrote to the governor of his state and asked him to send him a Florida flag to fly in Vietnam. "He always had a grin on his face," Phil remembers. "He loved to tell people that they had to do impossible things, and he'd make a joke out of it so it didn't seem quite so bad." His men loved him, Phil explains, because "he was more of a guy than an officer. He didn't look down upon you in any way."

John Holton looked for responsibility the way some kids look for trouble. He liked to be in charge and he liked to be independent; even as a child, he managed to buy himself a lawnmower so he could earn his own spending money. His knack for leadership was bolstered by his charm and enthusiasm. He never asked his troops to do something that he couldn't do himself.

John Holton believed in the war wholeheartedly, and that conviction never wavered. He left junior college to enlist in the Army and was accepted into Officers Candidate School.

Holton's father, a former bus driver who had gone into business for himself, tried to talk his son out of going to Vietnam. "The war was being fought more for money than anything else," the father warned. But John's mind was made up; he wanted to go and fight. And he expected his men to feel the same way.

Terror, however, was what Woodall felt when Holton told him he was going to walk point into the hamlet of Hai Lang. The point man went first, like a scout; if he survived, he would provide covering fire for the rest of the platoon. It was obviously very dangerous, which is why the "cherries" were so often given the chore; they were the most expendable.

Woodall later wrote a poem about that day:

> *Point man, point man, hump real fast.*
> *Enjoy each breath, may be the last.*
> *Point man, point man, danger spot,*
> *Crazy when it's peaceful, dead when it's not.*

At the end of the poem, the point man survives:

> *Point man, point man, going insane.*
> *Don't see the glory, do feel the pain.*
> *Point man, point man, what can you do?*
> *Drink lots of whiskey, slurp lots of brew.*

Woodall felt confident working with Holton, but not as point man. He managed to become the platoon's radio operator instead, controlling the troop's one link to the outside world. "The radio was where it was at," he says. "That's where the real firepower of Vietnam was. You can keep all this Rambo shit; just give me a radio—that's where you got gunboats, artillery, medevacs, food, and support."

Through February 1968, Holton, Woodall, and the rest of Company A slogged it out on Highway One. They moved out at night to set up ambushes in villages. It rained constantly. If they were lucky, the soldiers found graveyards to sleep in; the reverence many Vietnamese feel for their ancestors usually ensured the men a quiet rest in that macabre setting. Woodall was becoming a grunt. "You learn to say 'Fuck it, Jack, it don't mean a thing.' Not only did you learn to say that, you had to believe it." It also helped if you convinced yourself that you were going to die. "It made dying go from being bad to being normal. If you didn't do that, you'd go berserk."

Like Holton, Woodall had joined the Army and gone to Vietnam because he wanted to fight for his country. Soldiers were good guys where he grew up; as a kid he spent Saturday afternoons watching World War II movies. "I wanted to be a football player or a soldier," he says. "I wanted to be a hero. War heroes, sports heroes, I think that was what I looked up to." But unlike Holton, Woodall soon became deeply disillusioned with the war in Vietnam. He still believed in duty, in honor, but, as he wrote to his father in April 1968:

> *I guess I'm bitter now, Dad. This war is all wrong. I will continue to fight, win my medals and fight the elements and hardships of this country. But that is because I'm a soldier and it's my job and there are other people depending on me, that's my excuse. That's all I have, theories and excuses, no solutions.*

Not long afterward, following six months of heavy combat, Phil Woodall finally earned a leave to Hawaii for R and R. He was looking for fun, and he wanted to fulfill Lieutenant Holton's request to bring back some of the Bacardi Light Rum that Holton loved.

The trip did not go well. Woodall, still only nineteen and often unable to get served in bars, spent a lot of time in his hotel room drinking Jack Daniel's and acting out firefights into his tape recorder. He would play both roles—the RTO, calling in information and coordinates, and also the officer at the rear. When he went out, it was with a "hippie-type" girlfriend hired from an escort service, whom he took to movies and discos. What Woodall remembers most is being dazzled by neon lights.

By the time he left Honolulu, it almost seemed a relief to return to Vietnam, to be back with people who understood what was going on. But the night he returned, Bacardi rum in hand, he found out that John Holton was dead. He sat up all night in a bunker staring into blackness that was splintered by lights of a different kind—the neon-green tracer bullets. And he cried. "Holton was my friend, always. He was the only guy I ever cried over. I was uncontrollable."

Today, Phil Woodall lives in Pineville, North Carolina, where he works as an insurance man by day and writes poetry by night. He uses his verse as a way of connecting with his Vietnam service, as a way of remembering the most significant time of his life. "Vietnam gave me an emotional strength that's helped me through," he says. "Looking back at what some people did when they were nineteen years old, and what I did, I have to believe my education was pretty substantial. Perhaps not conventional, but certainly substantial."

Phil sat down not long ago to write to John Holton, almost twenty years after his death, because "I just wanted to tell him he was my buddy." But when he finished his letter, he didn't know what to do with it. He called Federal Express and explained the problem; the company delivered Phil's letter to the base of Panel 53 West, the Vietnam Veterans Memorial, Washington.

Phil had been to the memorial when it was dedicated in 1982. "I love the memorial," he says, but his first impression was a melancholy one. "It was on the Friday night after Veterans Day. I had an emptiness and a loneliness that I could not believe. I met some buddies there and we got kind of drunk and I was very sad. I felt very small.

"Pretty soon, we went over to the Lincoln Memorial. It was like a religious moment. Maybe it was the funeral service we never had time to have."

Phil and his son, Richard, don't talk much about the war, but it was his teenager who asked him the most difficult question he's faced since he came home from Vietnam: "Were you good guys or bad guys?" Phil Woodall has finally found an answer for him: "Both."

At Dau Tiang, Uttermark and I flipped a coin to see who would go with the new unit formed out of our old platoon. He went with the new unit. Two weeks later he was dead—doing the basic job I would have been doing. His name is on this monument, I'm alive.

John Keegan

DAVID LOUIS STOLL

Corporal, Company B, 2nd Battalion,
327th Infantry (Airborne), 101st Airborne Division
SEPTEMBER 3, 1948–OCTOBER 27, 1967

To: David Louis Stoll, my brother
Born: September 3, 1948
Died: October 27, 1967

July 31, 1986

Dear David,

   The last time I wrote you was in October, 1967, shortly before we
found out you were killed. If you could only know how much we
have missed you since then and how much it hurt to lose you. There
hasn't been a day (well, not very many anyway) that I haven't
thought of you. That goes for the whole family.
   A lot of things changed in 19 years—your age when you died.
Evan, Diana and I have all married and have kids. I married Gary,
the only in-law you met, and he is now a Colonel in the Air Force so
my kids move around like we did. Mom and Dad got divorced in
1979 and Mom remarried and both seem pretty happy.
   Do you remember that water buffalo Dad gave you when he came
back from Clark AB in 1965? Well, you gave it to me to keep when
you went into the Army in 1966 and I've had it ever since. I figure it's
time to give it back to you now. Gary and I and kids are on our way
to Clark AB to live for the next 2+ years. That buffalo has been with
me through 18 moves and I saved it from the packers this week for
you. I want it to be remembered that you were a real person who
lived and was loved very much. Someday I'll see you again. Until
then. Lots of love, your sister,

Sally

———•———

DAVID LOUIS STOLL had been in Vietnam one week when he was
killed on his first combat mission. He had just turned nineteen.
His wisdom teeth hadn't even come in yet.
   There were four siblings, a year apart, in the Stoll family; David
was the youngest, Sally, the oldest. "I guess the main thing, when I

think about David, is that he was so cute," she says. "As a little kid he had sandy blond hair which he wore in a crew cut and he had freckles, real freckles. I think of a happy-go-lucky kid, laughing with a crooked smile and crinkly eyes. I think of him at the swimming pool doing dives and showing off for the young girls; I think of him wanting to take sips of beer from Mom and Dad when he was little; and I think of him telling me of his adventures in the Army and how he parachuted and rolled over and over."

David enlisted in the Army in 1966, shortly after graduating from high school in Clovis, New Mexico. It seemed a sensible option; it gave him a chance to be on his own, save some money (he was eager to buy a TR-4 sports car), and have his college education paid for by the GI Bill. He hadn't decided on a career but was interested in landscape architecture. Though his father had made a successful career in the Air Force, and though David's first choice was the Marines, the Army was where he ended up.

"The Army was really good for David," says Sally. "It gave him that little chance to grow up that he needed." He was clearly proud of the Army, and Sally noticed that when he came home on leave, her brother seemed more mature, more serious.

He was ordered to Vietnam as a replacement several months ahead of his unit from the 101st Airborne. Before leaving, he made a point of zigzagging across the country to say good-bye to his relatives. "Naturally he'd be tense before going to Vietnam, but there was something about him, something there, that when I was with him my stomach just got tied up in knots and flip-flopped so much," says his sister. The whole family sensed it. Sally remembers trying to be positive, telling her mother, "Mom, there are statistics that prove you're safer in Vietnam than you are on the highway." But by the time David was waiting to board his plane at Denver's Stapleton Airport, the tension was palpable. Sally tried to lighten his mood by slipping him a pack of cigarettes and a copy of *Playboy*.

David was in Vietnam such a short time that he never received any of the letters his family sent him, not even the one his mom wrote before he left the States so he would have something waiting for him when he arrived. What was waiting for him took place at Tam Ky.

"His unit drew fire and the point position was hit," Sally recounts. "They set up a machine gun to cover the guys that were out front so they could get back. David saw the guy who was on the machine gun take a hit, and he took over the machine gun, apparently successfully, and managed to cover those people who were out there. And then David took a hit. He died right there on the spot." For his heroism, David Stoll was awarded the Silver Star.

"To have expected a person like David to have gotten through a year in Vietnam was just unrealistic, because he would never have thought to protect himself," his sister now realizes. "He would have thought more of his job and put his job and duty first, himself last."

Several weeks after David left for Vietnam, the family was saying good-bye to him again. "He was sent back to us in a steel coffin. He had dirt under his fingernails. They'd put a little makeup on him, but otherwise he was perfect, there wasn't a mark on him, just a little bruise under his cheek. When we viewed his body—it seemed indecent that such a young kid should have been lost in a war that men made. I thought that surely anyone who saw or handled his body should have felt shock, outrage, and extra grief at that sweet and innocent childlike face."

Her brother's death was a turning point in Sally's life. "When I found out about David being killed, I was twenty-three. I didn't feel very vulnerable then; nothing bad had ever happened to me, really. It was really like the whole world changed. Losing my brother was like being hit over the head with a sledgehammer, saying, 'Everything you thought before just isn't true anymore. Everything you believed in and your hopes for the future, that's not the way it is going to be.'"

In her grief, Sally didn't want to hear about the war, or think about it. But soon the man she was dating was sent to Vietnam as a pilot. He flew 186 sorties, returned safely, and they were married. Sally remembers, though, that the sadness and fear were still with her.

"Every now and then I would get into this sort of mood and there wasn't anything I could do about it," she says. "I would just want to go off and be by myself for a while, or I would be in bed and I would think about David and just start to cry. I can't tell you how often that happened.

"If our country had made different choices," she went on, "he would be alive today."

Before their recent move to a base in the Philippines, Sally, now in her early forties, and her husband, an Air Force colonel, lived with their three children outside Washington, D.C., in Virginia. They had come there from Korea in 1983, and only a few days after arriving, they went as a family to see the Vietnam Veterans Memorial for the first time.

"We looked his name up in the guidebook and found the panel," Sally recalls. "I certainly can remember vividly searching for it there, and then that moment of recognition. I felt scared seeing it, knowing all over again that it was real; that someone who was and is a part of me lives, in a sense, only chiseled in stone.

"I thought about him at nineteen, who he was then and what he might have become. I thought of his age in 1983—it would have been almost thirty-five, the age of many of those bright people in Washington offices.

"We stood in the sun and took some pictures of the panel and close-ups of his name. I didn't break down or sob or anything like that—just slow tears hidden behind sunglasses. I really wanted to tell someone else why we were there, or even announce to the world: 'See what happens when we, as a country or as a family, don't care enough about young, vulnerable lives?' "

It was the first of many visits to the memorial. But she had never gone there alone until she went with the carved wooden water buffalo and the note for her brother on the day before she was to move away from Washington. Many years ago, a life ago, David's father had brought the buffalo for his son from the Philippines; David had given it to Sally just before he entered the Army. It had followed her through eighteen moves in twenty years, and now that Sally was moving to the Philippines, it seemed the right time to give it back to David.

"It was like saying good-bye," she says. "When I left Washington, it was like leaving him and going away. Though David is buried in Indiana, I do feel his spirit is in that memorial. I feel a sense of closeness to everyone whose name is on there and to anybody who is a family member, close friend, or relative. There is a sense of unity about it that all those little separate gravestones scattered all over the country and the world don't seem to have. They're very private, and this is something where everybody belongs to us a little bit more."

She left her letter and the buffalo by David's panel and walked away. She did not linger, did not touch his name, did not let any emotion show.

The next morning, Sally started driving across the country to California with her children. She remembers the endless stretches of countryside in Kansas and Arizona, where it's always hard to find anything good on the radio. "You have a lot of time to think, and a lot of the thinking and talking I was doing with my children was about my family, and growing up. I really thought at that time that I could put David aside—not away, but I had a sense of completion."

That equilibrium did not last. Three months later, Sally's younger sister, Diana, died suddenly of an undiagnosed brain tumor. This second, inexplicable tragedy happened in October, the month of David's death. As she mourned the loss of her sister, she began mourning for her brother all over again. "It all comes back and it just about wipes me out."

When she went to Vermont for her sister's funeral, she found a scrapbook Diana had made about David. It contained every bit of memorabilia she could gather—all the clippings, all the letters. Sally learned from her brother-in-law how much Diana had cried over the years. Separated by distance and preoccupied with young families of their own, neither sister had realized how much the other was still grieving for their kid brother.

"The one thing that is very different about losing my sister at age thirty-nine and my brother at nineteen is that I know what my sister turned out like," Sally says. "Diana wasn't finished, she was still growing in different ways, but she did have a chance to have her own family. And David didn't.

"I always thought someday we would be grown up and visit each other with our kids and play cards in the evening, and it just hasn't turned out that way. I miss him, all the potential, all the things that might have been, and finding out what he would have been like as a grown-up person. I would have loved to see how he would have held a baby and taken care of a child of his own. That would have been a real joy."

To the Soldiers of the 101st Airborne:

In 1968 we spent some time together. We tried not to get close for reasons only you and I can understand, however we did. We laughed, drank beer, played cards and even cried together. Our camp was open to you and yours to us. I remember how safe I felt knowing we had you close by to help us get through those horrible nights. There were so many nights I watched the tracer rounds and mortars enter your camp and how helpless I felt wondering and praying we could make it just one day closer to our time to come home.

Terror was in the air, to this day I recall the smell and taste of it. The memories are the worst, from seeing Billy in tears and laying into his bayonet to the soccer game with a V.C. head. Billy was so scared he knew no other way out, and the game was the anger we all felt so much.

The worst memory for me is the day I sent the 76 men out of your 85 to their deaths.

I have to explain and I pray to God you will understand.

At approx 10:30am I watched tracer rounds from a 50 caliber firing upon a spotter plane. I knew no small group of V.C.'s would fire or carry the 50 cal. It wasn't a hit and miss outfit. I radioed in at about 10:45. By 11:00am the decision was made that you would go for the kill. As I helped and watched you ready for your mission, I recall saying "I'll see you ugly mugs for lunch." I had no idea you would never eat again.

As I watched the smoke and fire I felt good in thinking you men were really kicking ass and no names taken.

It wasn't until about 3pm that we found out you had walked into an entire regiment of North Vietnamese regulars. By the time the dragons came in it was too late. The B-52's closely followed and dropped their napalm on your position. The end of the war came for you. John and I guarded your empty camp that night hoping for stragglers, but no one came. It wasn't until the next day that we found out it was us they had wanted that night from a map found on one of the bodies. All 76 of you men died to save the 42 of us. Here are 76 fathers, mothers and God only knows how many wives and children left without you and I live with that thought every day of my life. Many times I have wished I had never seen those tracer rounds fired. To say I was sorry would be an added slap, but sorry I am. I will never forget my comrades and I will live with my guilt, sorrow, anger the rest of my life, my scars can't be seen or touched but they are deeper than any round that could have been fired. On Monday 11/11/85 I will say my goodbyes to you until we meet again.

Your Comrade
Ray, a Sea Bee

To the memory of Ronald G. St. John, 10 East, Line 104, and all others who died on September 16, 1966

The peace of the memorial belies the terrible hell of mud and fire where you fell, and since that day a whole generation has grown to maturity. Even so, friend, rest assured the flag yet flies at home, on summer nights taps still echo from Harrison's woods, lakes and hills, and on deep cold winter nights, the lake ice sings still.

Je me souviens.

J. Briggs
Major,
Infantry

In remembrance of Chris Peebler and D. J. Lipetzky
KIA June 1969 near Tam Ky, South Vietnam

Here you are my friend
Good to see you again.

Been awhile since we had to go
To the field, where the medal of honor grows.

Bronze and silver grew on trees
There for the pickin', just follow me

But our medals were made of lead
Not hangin' from our chests, in 'em instead.

But we're glad you're here. We knew you'd come
From Texas and Missouri it's a long run.

We're not lonely here, we've plenty of friends
Got 3 grunts lookin' over us, on guard till the end.

So don't fret your mind, don't shed your tears
Remember, we're here with you very, very near.

196 Light Infantry Brigade, Americal Division
We miss you all. Dan Dinklage and Jerry Feldman

EUGENE ALLEN HANDRAHAN

Sergeant First Class, Company A, 2nd Battalion,
12th Infantry Regiment, 25th Infantry Division
JULY 30, 1947–OCTOBER 10, 1968
Missing in Action

July 19, 1986

Dear Eugene,

We love you always, you are not forgotten. You have been a son we are very proud of.

You have healed the hurts of others and forgiven our faults.

Beyond the unknown there is mystery, beyond the faith there is a person, beyond the silence there is God. May he keep you in his loving care.

Love,
Mom and Dad

———•———

THEY WERE ONLY DREAMS, but they succeeded where the government failed, in providing Adeline Handrahan with peace of mind about her son Eugene, who had been declared missing in action in Vietnam eighteen years earlier.

It was Easter, several years after he'd disappeared. As Adeline slept, her own mother, dead for forty years, appeared to her. "I love you very much," her mother seemed to say. "The hand of the Lord has already touched." Adeline awoke with a feeling of deep contentment. "It meant to me," she says, "that Gene was dead. He was with God, and what more can we wish for? I knew he wasn't suffering at the hands of the Communists."

Her relief was confirmed by a dream Gene's widow had just a few days later. In it, Gene stood near the pearly gates and told his wife, "Sherri, don't worry about me. I am in heaven with my maker." For a devoutly religious woman like Adeline Handrahan, the two visions finally brought comfort.

Adeline raised six children in her small white house in St. Paul, Minnesota, and Gene was her first. "He was the happiest little guy —he would just sit in the high chair and smile," she says. He grew up to be an athletic, slightly bashful boy. "He never wanted to hurt anybody's feelings; he was happy-go-lucky."

By the end of 1967, Gene had a good job at a meat-packing plant and was engaged to his high school sweetheart. He was content, ambitious; and then he was drafted. He didn't want to go.

Joan, his younger sister, remembers how torn he was. "It was real uncomfortable to talk about," Joan recalls. "In one sense, you had to go because of duty. Dad had been in the Army. Also, we were brought up Catholic, and you're brought up to go; it's your patriotic duty to do this. But Gene was paying attention to the fact that guys were going to Canada. He had tough questions: Should I disgrace my family a little bit and go over the border? Or should I go off to war like my dad did and do my duty?"

Gene ultimately decided not to go to Canada, and in April 1968 he was sent to Vietnam; by then, he and his wife were expecting their first child. Thoughts of his family, and deeply held religious beliefs, seemed to sustain him. Seven months after he landed in Saigon, he wrote a letter to his mother in which he told her how thankful he was to be alive—that God was being good to him. But his luck was scuttled on October 10, when he served as point man for his platoon, then on patrol in the Cu Chi area, northwest of Saigon. Gene radioed back the words "I'm hit" and was never seen or heard from again.

His family thinks there are two possible explanations. The first is that he was captured and whisked into the tunnel system that the Viet Cong had built beneath Cu Chi to bring supplies into the Saigon region. The second possibility is that he was killed by American bombs, which raked the region after he was wounded but before there was an attempt to rescue him.

Under the merciless assault of time, the Handrahans have learned how cruel it is to be related to an MIA. "We're proud of him and his patriotism, but we are not proud of our government," says his sister Joan O'Brien, who has become an activist in the POW/MIA issue. She had been the Minnesota state coordinator for the National League of Families, but she recently left to join an offshoot group that focuses on the search for live POWs. Even though both she and her mother believe—and accept—that Gene is probably dead, they refuse to give up completely and remain committed to the painstaking, sometimes painful work. "If I wanted to do something fun," says Adeline, "I'd do something else."

Adeline Handrahan first saw her son's name on the Vietnam Memorial in July 1986, when she went with Joan to a National League of Families meeting in Washington, D.C. She wrote her note to Gene while attending one of the group's sessions; she still isn't sure why. "I just wanted to take him something," she says. When she finally got to the wall, its effect on her was consoling.

"It's inward, it's love, sadness—you really think about all these young guys and what they missed," she says, her voice trailing off. "If we could see a whole army of men like that marching . . . It's just too bad that we can't live and love each other and not have war."

For Joan, visiting the wall is like "walking through a tunnel of pain. Looking at all the names and picking up bits of conversations, you get the feeling for how many lives were touched. And I don't think you can balance the scales, the agony, the aftermath, and say it was worth it. They were so young. They found out what love and death were about at the same time."

Adeline no longer imagines her son coming home, but letters about him still find their way to Gene's old house on Montana Street. One woman wrote recently from a U.S. base in Germany to say she has been wearing Gene's POW bracelet for eighteen years; she wanted to know a little bit about him. Adeline sent her a picture of her son, touched that a stranger would still care.

The family remains close, and Adeline sees Gene's daughter, Pamela, born just before he vanished and now a Bible college student, as often as she can. On weekdays, she cares for another grandchild, and when she finds the time, she paints or does needlepoint —a needlepoint picture of the Last Supper hangs in her kitchen.

She doesn't dwell on the politics of the past, but her views have changed somewhat. Had she known, for instance, that the men who went to Canada would one day be given amnesty, she would have urged Gene to cross the border too. "At the time, I really thought it was his patriotic duty, but now I've changed my mind," she says. "I still love my country, but I think the government should stand behind its men. I used to have a lot more faith in the government than I do now."

This wedding ring belonged to a young Viet Cong fighter. He was killed by a Marine unit in the Phu Loc province of South Vietnam in May of 1968. I wish I knew more about this young man. I have carried this ring for 18 years and it's time for me to lay it down. This boy is not my enemy any longer.

Frederick Garten, Sgt. USMC

Hello Wayne,

I am terribly sorry that I haven't written sooner to you. Brother, you have been in my total thoughts the last twenty years. I wish I could hold you and tell you I love you. Blood, when those 'Cong opened up with the 50 caliber machine gun, we brought some on their ass, the cannon was kicking out HEP and cannister rounds, the 50 and 30 were spitting death. I am not very good at this, because I am crying my eyeballs out as I write now, you don't know it, but you gave the ultimate love for another human. Ruben Abril and Albert Beam and me are living because you took that Chi-Com. The last time I heard from Ruben in 1973, he was doing great. He is married and has two children. Ruben and I talked about you; the hurt rips my chest open and exposes my heart.

All the brothers that didn't return home from Operation Starlite are enshrined in Marine Corps history. They have a wall with your name on it, tens of thousands of Americans came to honor you and the rest of the brothers. And they have a three fighting man statue standing vigil over the wall. The statue is a fire team walking point for the wall.

The country is starting to open its eyes. They had two "Welcome Home" parades on May 7, 1985. I couldn't make the parade, but another brother from 3rd Recon marched for us, Wayne. Tim said there were millions of people there, the swarms of crowds yelled "We love you boys" for what you did and "Welcome Home." It was a very moving experience. They threw ticker tape. All the brothers cried for the brothers that didn't come home.

I got to go now. I know they buried you twenty years ago, but I am just now doing it. I promise every time I am in Washington, D. C. I will come to our wall and talk to you. I love you and goodbye.

"Brothers of the Bush"

Jim (Semper Fi)
C Co., 3 Tank Bn.
Chu Lai, Vietnam

Vietnam Veterans Memorial
Summer 1986

> *by Robert S. McGowan*
> *Co. A, 2nd BN, 8th Cav., 1st Cav. Div.*
> *Co. A, 1st BN, 501st Inf., 101st Airborne*

Aghast—
The ghosts emerge
> *through the woodline*
> *through the years*
Emerge tentatively
> *through a tear in time.*

Eyes
The eyes of boys
> *who have stood at the precipice*
> *who have looked into the dragon's maw*

Stare
> *from the woodline*
> *to a scar of granite on the nation's soul*
Where those touched
> *touched the names*
> *and see their own eyes*
> *looking back at them—*

The ghosts emerge
> *Exhausted*
> *Somber and aghast*

Dear Jesus
> *Is this*
> *What everything*
> *was for?*

Aghast
> *The ghosts' eyes see*
> *A frozen tidal wave*
> *Of grief and loss.*

In special memory for: Ssg. Anderson, Memchick, Saldana—
> *1st Abn Brigade, 1st Air Cav (65–66)*
> *Bogart Floyd, Gary Scott, Gary Hadley—*
> *2nd Bde, 101 Abn (67–68)*

Understand
That if the time comes
When you must kill
It will destroy you
For all of this life.
This is the horrible legacy
  of glorifying war
Which no one escapes
Who is the deadliest
Adversary;
    The soldier
    The truth
    or the monument?

WILLIAM PAUL MASON

Private First Class, Company D, 16th Armor,
173rd Airborne Brigade
APRIL 12, 1947–MARCH 4, 1968

DOUGLAS ALLEN HENNING

Private, Company B, 3rd Batallion,
506th Infantry (Airmobile), 101st Airborne Division
AUGUST 3, 1947–JULY 17, 1968

GARY RAY TOWNSEND

Lance Corporal, Company F, 2nd Battalion,
5th Marine Regiment, 1st Marine Division
JUNE 8, 1947–SEPTEMBER 30, 1968

Dear Gary, Doug and Billy,

Well, that time has rolled around and the Class of '65 is having its 20th year reunion. Cheers, cheers for Old Orchard Park High School.

Don't be afraid that you will not be remembered. We all talked about you in 1975 and our thoughts are with you. I think of you all —often.

Doug—they moved your house off the boulevard onto a new street. Your death was a real shock, especially since you were so adamant about hating guns.

Billy—I'm sorry that we never lived out the fantasy of running into each other in a supermarket with batches of children.

And yes, Gary, I still talk too much.

I had to come. I live in Los Angeles now and I could not have gone to that reunion without first coming here.

After you all died, I guess two boyfriends and several friends gone was a bit too much for me and I pretty much screwed up for ten years.

Two boyfriends is just too much, too much, too much.

Now I'm much better. More responsible. I learned that the pain and loss never goes away. It just changes. Sometimes I think it is more painful now. And I'm still mad.

All three of you hold a special place in my heart. I'm just sorry you had such little time to spend here.

> *Years later*
> *I can never hear*
>   *the sound of a helicopter*
> *Without remembering*
> *What I have lost.*

> *In leaving today*
>   *tears stain*
>   *the window of the airplane*
>   *on the runway.*
> *It has not rained*
>   *in L.A. for months*
> *It rains today.*

I have had
twenty years
now
to reflect on this
madness
And it is
always the same.

Linda Phillips Palo

Thinking of you,
Linda

———•———

LINDA PHILLIPS PALO remembers her hometown of Orchard Park, New York, as a splendid place to grow up. The conservative, Waspish Buffalo suburb was a place of traditional values and expectations in 1965. Linda felt she had it all. "We were children without turmoil. It was this idyllic little town, picture perfect. The world was going to be our oyster, this is what we were told. I could see a great decade, great things."

Linda, like her friends, knew exactly what was expected of her. "You get into the best school you can, marry the best guy you can, as fast as you can. We were training to be wives."

Gary, Doug, and Billy were Linda's friends—the all-American boys who were going to marry the all-American girls and raise children and mow lawns in happily-ever-after land.

Just the memory of Gary Townsend still makes her laugh. He and Linda, two of the school's brighter students, did not always apply themselves and ended up sitting together in a reading-enhancement class, where they needled the kids who actually were slow readers. They finished the year's curriculum within several weeks, and mocking it became a constant source of amusement. "Gary would come in and say, 'Well, have you read the story about the cow and the Chicago fire?' And I would answer, 'Of course, it's a must!' "

William Mason, Billy to his friends, knew how to get a good time going; his warm, extroverted personality assured him plenty of pals.

He was a boy who chose lemon meringue pie for his birthday instead of a cake and gobbled down raw oysters when given the chance. He loved life, and girls, like Linda, loved him.

One night, she and her friend Judy hid in the bushes outside Bill's bedroom window; it was one of the most daring things they had ever done. "He was putting away his wooden airplanes and he was dressed in just his jockey shorts and his shirt," Linda says. "We flipped, our hearts were pounding. It was almost like we weren't virgins anymore."

Doug Henning and Billy were best friends. "He practically lived at our house," said Billy's mother, Mary Mason, "and I remember how loving he was, how nice." Everyone agrees that Doug was, as the yearbook said, "the most fabulous defensive end in the history of Orchard Park." His nickname was Tony Tiger and his looks had teenage girls dreaming of true love. Doug and Billy's dream was to escape the Northeast someday and open a camp for city kids in the Colorado Rockies.

But the Vietnam War intruded on this perfect town. It became a ritual—before someone went off to war, the gang from Orchard Park High School would gather at the local pizza place to talk, drink beer, and try to be supportive. In Linda's church, departing soldiers were called to the altar and given a Bible to take with them to Vietnam.

When he was unable to get into the Air Force, Doug enlisted in the Army. He was determined to fight communism, and he joined the 101st Airborne. Bill, like Gary, had started college, but toward the end of his freshman year, he got his draft notice. Rather than take a college deferment, he joined the Army; like his best friend, Doug, he chose the 101st Airborne Division.

Bill's father tried to talk him out of it. But he told his father, "You and six of my uncles served when you were called during World War Two, and I have every intention of doing the same. It's now my turn."

He became a medic. Four months after he arrived in Vietnam, his mother had a nightmare. "Bill was in a fire, and he was calling me." It turned out to be the night he died. Billy Mason ran into a burning tank to rescue a buddy; as he was pulling him to safety, the tank was hit by a rocket and he died in the flames.

When he found out that Billy had been killed, Doug Henning was already in Vietnam. He immediately wrote to his parents that if anything happened to him, he wanted to be buried next to his best friend. Four months later, Doug's company was caught in a firefight at night. Doug was moving through the darkness to rescue a wounded soldier when a flare was ignited—either from a plane or by the point man—and on the illuminated battlefield he was instantly spotted and shot dead.

After losing his friends, Gary found his sociology classes at Colorado State less relevant. He decided to leave school and enlist in the Marines. Shortly after landing in Vietnam, Gary and the rest of Company F came under a heavy barrage of fire in Quang Nam province. Gary detected the North Vietnamese bunker where much of the firing was coming from, and he moved close so he could fire directly into it. He was killed, and like Doug and Billy he received the Silver Star for heroism.

When Linda heard that Gary was killed, she screamed, then put her emotions on hold for the next eleven years. She did not cry. She became numb. The deaths of her three friends destroyed her expectations about life. "It was like clay doves being shot out of the water," she says. "I thought I knew what I was dealing with. I needed rules and there weren't any. I got very confused."

Still, she managed to finish college and get a master's degree in American studies from the University of Buffalo. She married, worked, and actively opposed the war.

Time passed. By the time the war ended, she had been to psychiatrists, but she still avoided confronting the pain and depression she felt over her friends' deaths. One morning she felt so bad she couldn't get out of bed. That day, she asked her husband to give her a year—she would go to California to start a career in the movies. She went to San Francisco because, with only four hundred dollars, she didn't have enough money to buy the car she would need in Hollywood.

It was 1979. "I was thirty-two years old," she says. "I knew I had no time for entry-level jobs."

Linda got lucky. Hours after she was told by an entertainment-industry employment agency that they had nothing for a secretary with a master's degree, Francis Ford Coppola called looking for someone with precisely those credentials. She got the job. Coppola was completing a movie called *Apocalypse Now*.

The woman whose life had been shaped by a decade of internalized pain about the Vietnam War was suddenly in the middle of a cinematic Vietnam extravaganza.

Not long after starting work, she sat in Coppola's screening room and saw *Apocalypse Now*. She was overcome. She had always imagined Vietnam in black and white, like World War II newsreel footage, but now here it was on the screen, in color, alive. "As soon as the helicopter sound was all over the room, I thought *this* is what they were hearing: *Fwack, fwack, fwack.* I'd think of them running out there under that sound, so afraid." The war was a reality for her in a way that had been blocked for a decade. She had tapped in to her own deep emotional well. When she got back to her apartment she cried and cried. "It was the beginning, like opening up a heavily locked door."

Linda, now a casting director in Los Angeles, has seen *Apocalypse Now* twelve times. But although it was a movie that made her cry, it was a song that made her realize she needed to go to the Vietnam Veterans Memorial. The ballad, "Trying to Find a Way Home," sung by Charlie King, reminded Linda of a song her mother and grandmother sang to her when she was a little girl, "Softly and Tenderly Jesus Is Calling." "Trying to Find a Way Home" is about healing. It goes in part:

> *Down at the monument*
> *Tolling the alphabet*
> *Faces reflecting in the dark polished stone*
> *Hoping you can't find the names that you know are there*
> *Names of the friends who can never come home*
>
> *And though no one speaks of it*
> *Searching the list of names*
> *You can't help but look for your own*
> *When you don't find it, you turn away silently*
> *Time to be heading back home.*

The refrain is a plea:

> *Come home*
> *Come home*
> *You who are weary come home*
> *Home to a country in need of healing*
> *We're waiting for you to come home.*

Linda knew she was weary, but finally ready to confront her pain. Just before her twentieth high school reunion, she went to the Vietnam Veterans Memorial. "I didn't know if I'd grow up or get a nervous breakdown," she says. "All I knew was that I was going to open up the hatch. It was terrifying."

She flew from Los Angeles to Buffalo, composing the poem to her friends on the plane. The next day, she took a flight to Washington, D. C., with her sister and brother-in-law, a Vietnam vet; she hadn't wanted to go alone.

At first, she walked along like any other visitor and made rubbings of her friends' names, but then the shell broke. "I put my hand up there and the wall felt cold, so I put my face up against it and these incredible sobs started," Linda says. "Once that happened, and I could lay my face against the wall and sob, it gave me my freedom. I wanted to put my face up against there to make things warm again."

Suddenly she had the urge to write her friends. She sat in the grass and wrote the letter that she left, with her poem, by Gary's panel. She spent time by each name, thinking and remembering different things.

It was difficult for her to leave the memorial that day. "It was like saying good-bye to someone you love—like at a funeral, you hate to see the coffin go into the earth because that's the last contact you'll ever have," she says. "You hate to let go.

"But I felt like I had closed one door—not to forget them, but the door of rage and anger was finally closed."

He was only what a brother can be,
 always teaching, sharing and laughing with me.
Then came his decision to go away,
 and I still remember how he looked that day.
He walked straight and stood tall,
 as he answered his country's call.
He wasn't a hero or especially brave
 but he didn't stand on a corner and rant and rave.

Cowardice and lies he couldn't stand,
 for he was an American, a soldier and a man.
He had always done what he thought was right
 and evidently he thought Vietnam was our fight.
In a village so far away, I'm not sure of the name,
 he died as he had lived without any shame.
I hope more boys can grow up like him,
 for he was a man; my brother Jim.

     K. Amis, Colorado Springs, Colorado
     for my brother, Sp4 James Foley
     KIA February 24, 1966

Behold the Empty Place
Eugene S. Hunt

I called my God in question
    Lord, how can this thing be?
To let the wicked woodsman
    Cut down this precious tree
Thou could have took an older tree
    That wind and time had worn
Why take this young and perfect one,
    That never fruit had borne?

On whispering wings of silent thought
    My God then answered me,
Who told thee that the Woodsman
    Had harmed our perfect tree?
I've had this tree transplanted,
    Removed it from thy face
Look to where the young tree stood
    Behold the empty place.
Yes, I have land more suited
    For such a wondrous tree
And one so full of promise
    I wanted close to me.

(In loving memory of Donald R. Miller, KIA Vietnam 1968)

Basilio Gomez

Two hours have passed and still I have no words to say. I was too young to know and remember in 1968. I was a year old then. Now I am 19 years old. All I know is what I hear and see about my dad through pictures, clippings and memories from those who knew him. As I grow older I know more and more about him. I'm proud to be his son and he would be proud of me, his son. Well, what do you know? I also joined the service (Navy). Why? To do what my father did—protect this great country of ours for democracy and freedom.

With love,
Basilio Gomez, Jr.

JOSEPH KELLY HOLLINGSWORTH

Private First Class, Company B, 3rd Battalion,
1st Infantry Regiment, 23rd Infantry Division (Americal)
June 2, 1945–April 19, 1969

A Loving Tribute to the Memory of :
Joseph Kelly Hollingsworth,
Our Fair-Haired Son

He gave his life doing a job that
demanded sacrifice and dedication.
He went forth, knowing that the risk was
Great, and served with faith and determination.
He was not asked if he wished to go
But was told he must.
He did not ask if the cause was worthy,
If the cause was just.

"There is a God" said he, "that truth
I must defend.
Our country needs men, men on whom
It can depend.
Other men are going. Some are dying there.
I must go and strive for peace and show
the world I care."

The world still waits for the peace for
which he died,
Still waits for its sweet refrain.
We pray to God that our son, and
others like him, did not die in vain.

No tears came to ease our sorrow
It seemed our hearts were turned to stone
We could not believe, would not believe,
that our fair-haired one was gone.

As we walked behind his flag-draped casket,
the blue skies smiled down from above
Each bright ray of soft spring sunshine
seemed to say "All is well. God is love."

A tender youthful bugler blew "Taps"
Sweet plaintive notes echoed across the hill
The stars and stripes we held to our hearts
As a host of friends stood hushed and still.

With aching hearts we left him there
  where sweet wild flowers grow,
Where golden sunbeams kiss his roses
And gentle breezes blow.

Where mighty oak trees spread their branches
And stately pines reach toward the sky
Soothing raindrops caress the grasses
And lovely songbirds fly silently by.

As our tears flow we lift our heads
And with pride we hold them high
For faith and courage filled the way he trod.
We lift our hearts, too, for well we know
  that joy and peace are his
  because there is a God.

  Oneita W. Hollingsworth (His Mother)

———————•———————

MISS ONEITA was seventy-three years old before she traveled in an airplane for the first time, and when she did, it was to fly to Washington, D.C., to see her son's name on the Vietnam Veterans Memorial. "I was appalled," she says. "I was stricken with, well, grief, when I saw name after name. I realized that behind each name there was a sad story, a sad home, brokenhearted parents, children, and wives."

The poem she left as a tribute to her son Joseph was one she had composed in 1969, just months after his death in Vietnam. "I was writing about him, not to him," she says. "But that poem unloaded my heart."

For as long as anyone remembers, she's been called Miss Oneita by her neighbors and friends in Gloster, a small smudge of a town in southwestern Mississippi where she taught school for forty-two years. She's been married for over half a century to James Hollingsworth, a warm and rugged man whom most folks call Mr. Bilbo. They live on land that has been in the family for nearly a hundred years. Miss Oneita's ancestors called this part of Mississippi home for longer still. "This community is so much a part of us," she says; the old expression she quotes, "We have a church on every corner," isn't far from the truth.

To get to the Hollingsworths' you swerve off the beaten track through small towns that today have video stores next to the Feed 'n' Seed and past groceries with signs like "Jesus Is Lord, Meat Counter Open." Cotton has been dethroned as king in these parts, an abandoned wooden cotton gin rots, gradually sinking into the earth. Just down the road, quiet, remote, and barely touched by 1986, is the snug little house Mr. Bilbo built with his own hands in 1943.

Two years later, twins were born to the Hollingsworths: Joseph and James. The boys shared a playpen, and it was there that their different personalities first emerged. "Jimmy could do all sorts of antics to make Joseph laugh," Miss Oneita says. "I'd have to take Joseph out of the playpen, because I thought he was getting overcome."

Miss Oneita taught Jimmy and Joseph in kindergarten and first grade; when they grew older, Mr. Bilbo took them hunting for rabbits, squirrels, and deer in the woods that reclaimed the cotton fields near their house. Jimmy liked cars, trucks, and science, whereas Joseph was "more literary-minded." *My Friend Flicka* and *The Voice of Bugle Ann* were two of his favorite childhood books, and he gradually grew fond of "historical novels, things that had long descriptions in them."

He was not a bookish boy, however. "My Joseph was a great lover of nature," his mother says. "He'd come in from squirrel-hunting and say, 'I wish you could have been with me and seen the beech trees, the colors in the woods.' " The simple pleasures have been the abiding ones for the Hollingsworths. "I was never privileged to have much of this world's goods, but I've enjoyed what I could get for free," Miss Oneita says. "We can see beauty in a lot of things that some people would not see. There is beauty in simplicity."

The boys grew up straight, tall, sharing a back bedroom and everything else in life through the first two years of junior college. Then James enlisted in the Marine Corps, and Joseph went to the University of Mississippi, where he studied political science until the draft caught up with him. He was twenty-three.

"He did not go eagerly," Miss Oneita says. "He went because he had no other choice. But he accepted it and seemed to want to put forth his best effort." Miss Oneita and Mr. Bilbo both had brothers who fought in World War II, and neither had reason to distrust their government. "I wondered why we were in the war in the first place," she says, "but we accepted the wisdom of those people who sent us there."

Joseph Hollingsworth left for Vietnam on New Year's Day, 1969. The departure was wrenching. "When he put his arms around me," his mother remembers, "I did not shed a tear. God helped me, because I knew what it would do to him if he walked away and left me weeping. We told him we believed in him and we'd be at home working and praying for him."

If Joseph felt any doubts or fears while in Vietnam, he never confided them to his parents. His letters home were always upbeat, so much so that the Hollingsworths had complete faith that he would return safely. But then, one Sunday morning in April, as they were getting ready for church, Miss Oneita saw military officers coming up her walk. "Please, don't tell us," she pleaded, but the couple was informed that one of their boys was dead. "Which one?" Miss Oneita cried. It was Joseph, killed by rifle fire south of Danang.

They didn't go to church that Sunday, but the church came to them. Their family and friends rallied round and buttressed them in their grief. Jimmy, who was not then stationed in Vietnam, came home too, and the family prayed. "We prayed for tears. The first reaction was shock," Miss Oneita says. "And when the tears finally came, they were hard to stop." It took ten days for Joseph's body to come home. The funeral was held in the Baptist church he had belonged to since he was placed on its cradle roll in 1945. "Beautiful Isle of Somewhere" and "Beyond the Sunset" were played on the organ, and then he was buried in the church cemetery across the street.

The top of his grave is covered with small pebbles of white marble. Jim Hollingsworth kneels there, letting the rocks run through his fingers over and over again. It is almost impossible for him to talk about his brother, but what he can't say in words is expressed in the tenderness of his gestures. He smooths over the pebbles, patting them, making them neat. He straightens the vase with the bright bouquet of plastic flowers and positions it at the base of the headstone, moving rocks around it so it will be less likely to tip over. On the tombstone is an oval metal case that says "Son," and Jim slides it over to look at the picture of Joseph, a strikingly handsome, serious boy in an Army uniform.

"There is no grief like losing a child," says Miss Oneita. "You never really get over it. It doesn't take much to cause depression to hit you like a ton of bricks. But you have to work at it. It takes a lot of hard work and praying and wishing and doing."

Still, neither Miss Oneita nor Mr. Bilbo feels any rancor about the war that killed their son. "We are not bitter, have never been bitter," she says. "We have been saddened and hurt and have often wondered why. We need a healing, our nation needs a healing, but bitterness has never healed anything.

"When we say we lost the war, we are wrong. Because each man that put forth his best and did the very best he could under the circumstances was a winner. No one who does their best is ever a loser. The men that served in Vietnam deserve the same kind of honor, appreciation, and recognition as any men who served in any war in which our country was involved."

But when she braved an airplane for the first time to visit the Vietnam Veterans Memorial, it was to see and honor the name of one man—her son. "It struck me harder than I thought it would," she says. "It has a kind of beauty that stays with you. I was very touched by the statues of the three soldiers; now that brings tears."

She was struck, too, by the respect of the other tourists. "Everyone was whisperingly quiet. It was a place where you heard nothing except the walking feet and the low tones of voices." She was especially pleased that no man was honored any more than any of the rest, and that each man's sacrifice is respected and remembered.

Because Joseph's name is high up on the wall, a park ranger had to help her and her family make a rubbing; Miss Oneita took it, and left behind two small American flags and her poem. After they returned to their hotel, Jim Hollingsworth went back to the memorial and spent two hours there alone.

If, as Miss Oneita sometimes dreams, Joe Hollingsworth could come through her front door again, home would still smell like home. There is likely to be a ham in the oven and creamed corn on the stove; there will be potatoes au gratin and cinnamon pickles that Miss Oneita put up herself. There are butter beans and sliced tomatoes from the garden, biscuits and butter, pound cake and chess pie for dessert. Miss Oneita's life revolves around Mr. Bilbo, their surviving son, his wife and three children, and the Mount Pleasant Baptist Church. Her faith holds the promise of a reunion with her son in heaven, and it sustains her. "We have great hope for the hereafter," she says. "God will have a beautiful tomorrow. We'll be together again. We'll see him again. We have great hopes of that."

July 4, 1985

In memory of Jim Blakley, Angel Correa and Teddy Hart
1st Platoon, E Co, 2nd Bn, 4th Marines

On June 26, 1967, on a small hill near Camp Evans, along Highway
1, north of Hue, RVN, Jim Blakely never saw the mine he stepped on
that morning. Nor did he live long enough to feel the wounds he
would soon die from. The concussion of the mine's explosion
detonated a 60mm mortar round carried on the back of Angel Correa.
Angel never heard it. A piece of shrapnel caught Teddy (Doc) Hart in
the chest. Doc was gone before his knees buckled. An instant in time
for some, an eternity for others.

Rest in peace, my friends, we will not forget you.

Warren E. Howe
Star Prairie, Wis.

DONALD G. RESPECKI

Sergeant, Troop B, 2nd Squadron, 17th Cavalry,
101st Airborne Division (Airmobile)
DECEMBER 26, 1942–APRIL 12, 1969

I remember your elation the night we graduated from Gaylord High School together in 1960. You and I may not have been the "honor" students that night, but none were more excited about our future. You had chosen military service, I planned service to others through social work.

You gave your life for all of us. Now I'm just a middle-aged woman, working daily with people whose youthful dreams have been shattered by life.

I, and the Class of 1960, celebrating our 25 reunion this month, salute you, Don, and tell you we will never forget.

Jean Crawford Strickler

———•———

I AM not a member of his immediate family, I'm not his mother, but in a way, I'm like one of his sisters," says Jean Crawford Strickler. "What you have in the town and the community where we grew up is a kind of extended family. His death was the first break in the circle."

Jean Crawford Strickler and Don Respecki were raised and went to high school in Gaylord, Michigan, a tiny town with Bavarian-style buildings on Main Street and a good-natured friendliness that breeds nostalgia in those, like Jean, who move away. "Gaylord is a good place to grow up," she says. "The people there are down-to-earth. The climate is on the rough side—people have to work hard, and work is a very important part of life. It was a small enough town that people knew everybody and they looked after each other."

Jean and Don were two of the fifty-five graduates in Gaylord High School's class of 1960. Many had been together since kindergarten; the entire student body ate lunch together in the same dining room at the same time.

Most of the classmates had been born in 1942, part of the generation that preceded the baby boomers. For them, adolescence was still a carefree time. Girls wore their cardigan sweaters buttoned down the back and wrapped inches of angora wool around their boyfriends' class rings to make them fit their own fingers. Jean still remembers how funny it was when some of the boys from her class crashed a slumber party wearing purloined baby-doll pajamas.

They were fifties kids, reared on Elvis and Eisenhower. Don's mother, Georgia Respecki, recalls ironing while her small house on Ohio Street was jolted with the sounds of "Blue Suede Shoes" and "Jailhouse Rock"; Don and his best friend, Tony, would practice dancing, and sometimes Georgia would even put down her iron to join them as the music took over the house.

Jean and Don saw a lot of each other. Often they'd meet in the principal's office in the morning to get a note excusing their lateness. They also attended dances and showed up together at the one movie theater in town, which showed films on Saturday night. But they never went steady. "We liked each other—I liked him a lot," she says. "But I was not in a position where I was considering any serious relationships. Not in high school, and not in college, because I had a lot of desire to make something of myself." Her sentiment was unusual in a girl; Gaylord High School's principal thought it was a waste of time for them to go to college.

Yet Jean did continue her education, while Don Respecki went off to Detroit to get a job. The hardworking kid who had bought his mother a Sunbeam Electric Frying Pan with money from his first newspaper route was eager to settle down into his life as a hardworking man. Eventually he landed a job with Ford in the parts department, and that delighted him. He had a start in the industry he thought could provide him with security.

Then he was drafted. The bad news came shortly before he turned twenty-five. He was registered not in Detroit but with his local draft board in Otsego County, and they were looking for men. By the end of 1967, there were 500,000 Americans in Vietnam, and Don Respecki found out he was going to be one more.

He completed basic training in the spring of 1968 and came home on leave before shipping overseas. His fear, he told his mother, was that his fellow draftees seemed so young and immature. "If I never come back," Don said, "it will be because of these greenhorns that don't know what they are doing." When they took Don to the airport to see him off, Georgia Respecki wore her brightest yellow dress so her son would be sure to spot her when he waved good-bye from the plane.

Within a year, by April 1969, Don was dead, a casualty of friendly fire. Jean had just married and was pregnant with her first child.

It was a rough time for her. Her father had been killed in an airplane crash, and the person who had been the best man at her wedding, a Vietnam veteran, had committed suicide. When she heard about Don's death her feeling was: And this too?

"I didn't deal with it at first. I put those kinds of things on hold. I was encouraged to do that." Because she was pregnant, she was not supposed to get upset; she was even dissuaded from going to the best man's funeral, and she never really considered going back to Gaylord for Don's. It would be years before she confronted her feelings about his death.

Georgia Respecki, though, could not attempt such distancing. It was springtime and her spirits had been high. Don would be home in seventy days—she was counting. He had been moved to the rear and wrote that he would no longer go out on combat patrols; Georgia felt so relieved by that. "I had been in the Pendleton shop and picked out a new sport coat for him," she remembers. "It was a blue-and-white houndstooth check with a little bit of wine red in it. It was forty dollars and I thought, Should I wait until he gets back or buy it now?" That afternoon, her minister knocked on her door. "Hi, come in, what can I do for you?" she asked cheerfully. But a moment later, she knew.

Two days after she learned of Don's death, a letter arrived from him. She tore it open, praying there'd been a mistake. But the note was dated before his death; it wasn't a reprieve.

Dear Mom,

You sure have a sense of timing. The package arrived Easter Sunday. The sauerkraut and kielbasa is number one. I had two guys helping me eat it at the same time. On Easter Sunday, I got transferred to the infantry section, so I've already been out humping again. I'll never believe anything unless they put it in writing. They told me I wouldn't have to go out again. There's only about six or seven of us who know anything about what's happening.

Just opened some Cheez-its, tasted pretty good. It's 8:30 now, so I'll turn in pretty soon. Not much more to say Mom. Maybe have more news next time. Take care, Love, Don.

Eighteen years after his burial, Georgia Respecki talks of her son in a voice so quiet it verges on prayer. "It is still very real, it is still very near, and it is still very overwhelming," she says. "He was far away from home. He was where nobody loved him. He was where nobody could care for him. There was nobody near. He was a tender little boy, a loving little boy."

The Army told her very little about the circumstances of his death; in reading the generic condolence letters and terse cables, one senses that the Army would have preferred to tell all families simply that their sons had been killed by "bullets" and leave it at that. The telegram to the Respeckis said Don was killed "by fragments when an artillery round directed at a hostile force landed in the area." She wrote to the Army for more details but received a second form letter.

She is not bitter. "What good would it do? It won't bring Don back." Today, she dwells instead on the little boy who drank the juice from a dill-pickle jar, had a hound dog named Freckles, and sang "O Holy Night" in church when he was twelve. She's still touched and surprised that on the day he was buried, many shops along the funeral route were closed and many flags were flying. The town had lost a son, too.

The year after Don's death, the class of 1960 held its tenth reunion. The controversy over Vietnam had seeped into small towns like Gaylord, and the alumni were divided into hawks, doves, and people who, like Jean, felt the war was wrong but kept their opinions to themselves. A rift quickly developed when several of the more "radical" graduates said they thought it had been a mistake to spend money from the class fund for a wreath for Don's funeral. Jean was greatly upset, and it was her sadness over the divisiveness that eventually motivated her, fifteen years later, to go to the Vietnam Veterans Memorial and leave her letter for Don.

"My purpose was to complete a circle that had been broken by forces outside ourselves," she says. "I was saying, We miss you. We have never stopped loving you in the way we always did. I was saying, I know there was division at the time of your death, but it is going. Don was one of the good guys and you don't want the good guys to die. He was a real person. He was honest and a good friend."

As do so many visitors, Jean felt a sense of spiritual connection at the wall. "I felt in some way that Don was standing in front of me," she says. "I could visualize him very clearly—and I'm not a hysterical person at all. I really think that that's the beauty of the memorial. It seems to be a place where you can evoke feelings like that. It's open.

There is not a lot of false emotion involved. It reminds me of Japanese poetry, haiku—it's just the bare skeleton; you have to bring your own thoughts."

Now living in Lansing, Jean has an eighteen-year-old daughter and works as a vocational rehabilitation counselor. She has changed a lot since she left Gaylord, and part of that chage is due to Vietnam. "I am less conservative. I am not a radical but I am more suspicious about what really happens in making the decisions that shape all our lives," Jean says. "I am not less of a patriot, but I am less naïve and trusting and I think that is good.

"The war, I feel, was such a terrible waste—there wasn't any real reason for any of it. But I separate the politics from the people who fought; I never, ever blamed them. I blame the people that never had to go near the place. I would feel a lot better if we had learned something from it, but instead, we turned on people, the ones who went, the people who had the least control. And we turned on each other. It isn't completely over yet."

Except perhaps in Gaylord. A few weeks after she left her letter at the wall, Jean Strickler returned to her hometown for her twenty-fifth class reunion. The classmates who had been so divided at their tenth reunion, when they were all about twenty-eight years old, were now forty-three. Their children were about as old as Don had been when he died.

When Jean opened her reunion booklet, with its pictures and brief biographies of members of the class, she was startled to see Don's photo on the first page. Above it were these words: "We dedicate this program to our classmate, Don Respecki, who gave his life in the service of his country." Jean was not the only one who had come to terms with Don's death.

Some don't understand why I can't let it go, but you and I know. We could depend only on ourselves, we took care of each other. Our trust in one another was absolute, even if it meant personal sacrifice. We shared experiences and emotions that can never be expressed with words. You just had to be there, man.

Coming back to the world was a bitch! Years of foul accusations, stereotyping, lack of respect and not being accepted back into the mainstream of society. However, I dealt with it by using something I had learned in Viet fucking Nam. I just turned on the ol "fuck it" attitude. Something harder to deal with is you're not here. Perhaps the problem is that some say you died in vain. You did nothing in vain, man. They did! They have no idea of who you were, what you were doing or what you were trying to do.

You gave your life for all of us, man. I wouldn't leave you there alone. You are me and I am you. I will always remain "on guard duty." You and I know why I can't let it go.

—Rick Rogers
Wichita, Kansas

4th Logistics Command,
3rd Military Police Battalion,
Marine Security, 15th Army
Advisory Group, MACV

Dear Billy,

Well, I finally made it to say goodbye! Sorry it took 16 years, but you know how hard it is to say anything for me.

You can't believe how much things have changed. No more long hair, no more VW vans with flowers. But I guess we missed out on most of that when we went over to beautiful Vietnam in '69.

Your name is on a black wall in D.C., but I'm sorry to say that it's a little below ground—kind of like how Charlie was! You look over a nice green—a place like we used to play football on back home. A lot of people walk by all day—you can tell the Vets—we are the ones who don't have to ask about the size or type of material used to make the wall. We just stand and look, not caring who sees us cry—just like no one cared who died.

I just moved to Washington, D.C., from New York City. No, Billy, I never did make it as a writer. I gave it 10 years but now I'm 34 and I better get my shit together. I was married and I have 2 kids. A boy, Billy (guess who I named him after!!!), and a beautiful little girl, Sharon.

The day after you got it—I was hit in both legs and the back. Just my luck, I got the special ticket home and spent 3 years having operations and all that other shit that "recovery" means.

I miss our talks Billy—sometimes I get scared and no one understands how I feel. I guess only those who were there know the fear and pain that is felt.

I guess it's time for me to travel on, Billy. The light is going and my hand is shaking. I miss you, guy, and wish we could have laughed together for these past 16 years.

Take care, guy, and don't worry, I'll be back to visit. (Don't forget the 2 broads in the hospital!! What a time we had that night.)

Your Pal, "Shock"
Robert Shockley

Special orders to Billy Pedings, "Welcome Home."

MAURICE FREDERICK NORTHRUP

Private First Class, Company C, 1st Battalion,
327th Infantry (Airborne), 101st Airborne Division
MAY 12, 1946–NOVEMBER 8, 1967

When I was 5, we walked to school together. In the winter, he would drag his foot through the snow and make a path for me to walk in.

When I was 7, he'd get mad at me because I used to tease him so much. I remember once he was hitting me, we were on the corner, a man stopped his car and yelled "Stop hitting that little girl!" I said, "Oh shut up mister, he's my brother and he can hit me if he wants to."

When I was 10, Mom and her boyfriend would argue. I'd get scared and cry. Donnie would push my head against his chest and tell me not to worry, it would be alright.

When I was 14, he showed me how to walk like a boy, in case I had to walk home alone at night.

When I was 15, he'd quit school. He'd take two busses out to a big supermarket in the suburbs to bag grocerys to help Mom buy our food. He gave me three dollars to buy a pair of shoes, because I told him how much they looked like Capezio flats.

When I was 16, he got us our first phone. He gave it to me for my birthday. He brought Morris home that year too. He asked Mom, "Can Morris stay with us? . . . He's been sleeping in an old car."

When I was 17, Donnie and Morris joined the Army.

When I was 19, he came home on leave. He told me he was going to Vietnam. I started to cry. He pushed my head against his chest and said he was only kidding.

When I was 20, Mom got a telegram. June, our neighbor called me at work. I got cold all over. "June, open it! Is it Donnie?" "No, thank God, it's Morris." Oh God, I'm sorry Morris. It's okay, he's only wounded. Three days later another telegram. Morris is dead, shrapnel in Nam. No, Donnie, you can't come home for the funeral, Morris was only your foster brother, not a blood relative.

The war is real now, not just on T.V. news. My brother could die there!

When I was 21, Donnie came home. Tony, my husband, doesn't have time to stop the car before I'm out and running. I am so happy! But Donnie looks pale and nervous.

I am 22, Donnie is different, he stays in his room all the time. Mom calls, she's crying, he won't talk to her at all.

Donnie has a skin cancer removed from his shoulder.

I am 23, I see Donnie every day now. He gives me a ride to work and drops my son off at the babysitter's. Don's better now, more like his old self. He's got a good job driving a truck.

I am 25, Donnie's met a girl, Ann. I think he loves her. She's good for him.

I am 26, Don and Ann are married now. He's going to be a father.

I am 29, Don and Ann are having a hard time. They have a little girl, Leslie Ann. Donnie loves her very much.

I am 32, Don and Ann are divorced. He sees Leslie every day.

I am 35, I can't stand this. It's the most awful thing I've ever heard in my life. "Tony, come home, Donnie just called me. He says he has cancer in his jaw."

Don and Ann decide that he should go to the V.A. Hospital. The doctors there say "Let's wait and see what we can do. You're too young to have this or this type of surgery. Let's see if we can save most of your jaw." Ann calls, Missy, come pick us up. Donnie can come home. He's going to have radiation before surgery. He can do that as an out-patient. They've locked up his clothes for the night. Don says he'll take the bus if he has to, even if he is in his pajamas. I pick them up, we're all laughing. He's free! We feel like we've just busted him out of jail.

The doctors pull most of his teeth. They tell Don if he gets a cavity, there wouldn't be any way to fix it because of the radiation.

We can see the tumor now.

The radiation is working. He can't eat, his mouth is on fire. There's no saliva. His beard will never grow back. He's so thin.

Donnie has added his name to the Agent Orange suit.

I see him every day. I can't stay away. I know it sounds awful, but I had to see him. I always felt better after. He's going through hell but he makes me feel better.

It's October, Don has surgery today. No one knows what to say. Donnie's joking as they close the elevator doors. Mom, Dad, Steve, Ann and I are all numb. The doctors removed about an inch and a half of jaw bone. That's not so bad is it?

Put your fingers up to your jaw and measure.

Oh, God, how could you let this happen to him?

Donnie's home and doing fine. It's going to take a long time to heal, but he's young and in good shape. He's going back to work. He can't taste food but maybe the taste buds will come back. He carries a little water bottle with him wherever he goes. His mouth is dry all the time.

The company he works for is going out of business. Another company is going to hire the help.

Don's out of a job. The dispatcher keeps sending Donnie out to move stoves and refrigerators. Donnie tells him that he can't do that kind of work anymore because his arm isn't strong enough since his surgery. (This company knew this when they hired him.) The dispatcher says, "Either go out on the job or walk." Donnie walks. The next day, the president of the company calls and says he's sorry, it won't happen again and please come back to work. Donnie goes and every day they say, "Sorry, Don, no work today!" After three weeks he doesn't go back.

It's been about a year since his surgery. Don's got this hole in his cheek, it's never healed up, pus runs out of it. The doctors take Don back into surgery. It was only stiches that weren't removed from the first surgery. I'm so thankful it's not more cancer. I didn't realize someone didn't do their job right the first time around.

We all tell Don to file for disability. He finally does but his claim is denied.

He's been looking for a job now for two years.

I'm angry!

I called the Vietnam Veterans organization asking what I could do or where I could get help for my brother. They tell me it's hopeless. Only one veteran told me not to give up. "Keep trying," he said. "Not only for your brother, but for all of us. Tell them you're not going away."

I called the V.A. and talked to a Veteran Service Officer. He's supposed to be like a watchdog. His job is to see that all veterans get treated fairly. I told him about Donnie. He said he would look up his file and call me back. Finally, after two weeks, I learned that Donnie could file an appeal. However, he's sure it will be turned down. Then Don could file an appeal to the Board in Washington, and that too would be turned down. Both of these appeals taking about a year and a half. He also told me that the V.A. or our government's stand on this is: if you take any group of people, a certain percent are going to get cancer anyway. Well, that may be, *but almost half of my brother's face is missing and it wasn't shot off. The chemicals that our government told our men to use caused this soft skin cancer in my brother. He's been wounded, only not by the enemy.*

I never saw Donnie cry, the whole time he was going through radiation, before or after his surgery. But he cried when he had to take money from me.

He's losing his self-respect.

I realize that Donnie's not the only Vietnam Veteran in trouble, but he is the only one that's my brother.

Isn't anyone going to do anything about all these men? Has everyone forgot? Does everyone hope they'll all just go away?

At the very least, my brother and all the others like him deserve their self-respect, a job, and the right to live out the rest of their lives with the nightmares that war brings in some kind of secure peace.

I can't tell Donnie about this letter because what if that veteran is right! What if no one cares?

Sincerely yours,
Donnie's sister Missy

WHEN Nancy Mahowald heard that her foster brother, Maurice Northrup, had been killed in Vietnam, her first reaction was: Thank God it wasn't Donnie. Almost immediately she was overwhelmed by guilt, and for nineteen years she continued to feel bad about that response. "I knew it really bothered me. I'd be working around the house, thinking to myself, That's stupid. You were young then—it was a natural reaction to have at the time."

Donnie was the older brother she had looked up to all through her childhood. Maurice, known as Morris, was adopted by her family when he was a teenager. He and Donnie served in Vietnam at the same time.

Nancy Mahowald, now thirty-eight, is the kind of woman you'd like to live next door to. She is calm and smart and loaded with common sense. The Mr. Coffee pot is always full, and there is a plate of Dunkin' Donuts on her kitchen table. She lives on a small street in South Minneapolis, in a neighborhod where traditional virtues are still respected and where people have always believed in their government and sent their sons off willingly to fight its wars.

Nancy learned to question that belief because of Vietnam, and because of what happened to Donnie and Morris.

She had never been out of Minnesota and she had never been on an airplane until she went to the Vietnam Veterans Memorial; the trip was an offshoot of a conference her husband, a firefighter, had to attend. She remembers: "It was hard to get rid of the guilt. I didn't realize how much was there until I walked away from the memorial. When I turned and walked away, the guilt was gone. I felt relieved and quiet, quiet inside. I couldn't believe how peaceful I felt. I had the feeling, I've gone on a mission, I've done it. It's over.

"You just don't realize how many people died until you see the names. When you start walking down there and get to the apex and look up and suddenly realize you are standing there surrounded by all those names of people that died, it is overwhelming. I felt, Morris is there with all the other guys. He is not alone. It was easier for me."

Nancy brought her letter almost as an afterthought. "I packed the night before and I thought, Well, I'll take a copy of the letter and leave it for Morris. He and Donnie were so close. It sounds silly, because Morris is buried right here, at Fort Snelling, and I could have taken the letter there, but somehow it's not the same."

The letter had grown out of her anger and frustration about Donnie's battle with Agent Orange disease. She had done everything she could think of to help her brother, and finally she decided to write a letter. She worked on it for several weeks, and when she was satisfied, she mailed copies of it to thirty-five people—from state officials to country-and-western singers. Her hope was to focus attention on Donnie and others like him who, she felt, were being ignored. There was nothing she could do for Morris, but maybe, just maybe, she could make a difference for Donnie.

Morris and Donnie were "the guys." Morris was a Chippewa Indian, orphaned at an early age and farmed out to foster homes. He and Donnie met as teenagers and he soon felt so comfortable at the Mahowald home that he was invited to join it; when the paperwork was completed, it certified what everyone felt: Morris was one of them.

"The guys" seemed to have a better time out of school than in, and they both left high school before graduation. They tried to find decent jobs but couldn't; then they tried vocational school, but they didn't like that either.

Nancy remembers that her mother arrranged to have a tutor come and help the boys finish high school at home. The family was impressed with their cooperation and their seemingly smooth transition back into academic life. That lasted for about two weeks—until Nancy went into the boys' room unannounced during a tutorial session and discovered that the teacher's briefcase contained a six-pack and a deck of cards.

The Army seemed a possible solution. Maurice and Donnie hoped to be in the Special Forces together, but it didn't work out that way.

Morris wrote home to the Mahowalds from basic training:

> *I will be in the battle mostly all the time and when I think about it, I really get scared, so I try not to think about it, but the sergeants always tell us to kill anything that moves or breathes and we really have some powerful weapons so that helps. Our M-16, it's a rifle we will carry, if its bullet hit somebody in the knee cap it would disintegrate all his bones in that leg. . . . Then we have an M-79 that can destroy 200 men at 200 meters.*

Morris was twenty-one. Shortly before he left for Vietnam he married Sandy, who was the mother of his two baby boys, Maurice junior and Donnie. His dream was to save two thousand dollars while in Vietnam and then come home and go to trade school.

Morris's letters from Vietnam reflected the reality of the grunt's life:

> *I don't get sick when I see dead VC and some of them get pretty blown away. Matter of fact, I think it's kind of funny. (I must be getting hard core.) The only time I really get scared is at nighttime when I am pulling guard and let me tell you, I really get scared. My imagination runs away from me and I think I see shadows moving towards me and footsteps and everything. It's really weird. I'm really happy when morning comes along. . . . There sure are a lot of ants and flies here. The ants really bite hard, too. All the flies do is get in your sores and lay eggs. That happened to me before. NO MORE ROOM, Maurice.*

The first official telegram said that Maurice had been wounded by shrapnel near Chu Lai. The second cable said that he was recovering from his wounds, and the third said he was dead. It was November 1967.

Morris's death brought the war home to Nancy Mahowald, and she worried more about Donnie's survival, but she still did not question the war. She was a newlywed, and her patriotism was firmly rooted in the belief that what your government says is true.

Donnie did survive and came home from Vietnam quiet and moody. He had lost not only Morris but eight other friends as well. He didn't talk about the war, and he couldn't bring himself to visit Sandy, Morris's widow, and her two sons.

Twelve years later, Donnie learned that he had cancer in his jaw. Nancy watched the disease whittle away at her brother. It took part of his jaw, his sense of taste, his self-esteem. He lost his job and found he was not eligible for any disability payments. His medical bills were paid by the VA, but unless he wanted to claim mental-health ailments, which he didn't have, he wasn't entitled to any further assistance. One year, before Christmas, Nancy slipped him some money on the side. He broke down and cried for the first time.

"Do you know how painful it was to watch my brother? He couldn't even sell his house. He would have had to take out a loan just to pay the realtor's fees. When I think of how close we came to having him crawl on his hands and knees, I get so angry. Donnie is a good man, a kind man."

Nancy's unquestioning patriotism was gone. "Don't get me wrong, I love this country. I love it dearly, and I do think it's the best place to be. I just feel that something went wrong somehow, somebody got something screwed up. We had no business being in Vietnam.

"I'm angry at the way veterans have been treated since the war. And excuse me, how asinine people can be about the war! I can understand how I could be so stupid—I was young! But how can people in their fifties, how can they be so stupid about the war?

"I don't give a rip what anyone says or thinks of me. I know I'm okay. I love the country, but I feel deceived, that's where the anger comes from. I feel lied to. I feel stupid. That's where the anger comes from too."

Nancy knows it is impossible to prove conclusively that her brother's cancer was caused by Agent Orange. But she points out that the soldiers who fought in Vietnam did not ask the government to prove conclusively that the war was winnable or justifiable before they picked up their guns.

"I want the government to recognize what they have done and to say 'We're sorry this happened to you and we will take care of you.' I don't want them to give someone like Donnie nine hundred dollars a month to sit around for the rest of his life, but I want them to say they're sorry."

Nancy knows her children, Steve, sixteen, and Andrea, ten, have grown up with a different kind of patriotism. "They are patriotic but they are not blind. The difference is that I believed everything anybody having to do with the White House told me. I don't believe anything anymore. I think my children today are more intelligent than people my age were. I want my kids to question everything, to judge for themselves."

Morris's two boys are now twenty-one and twenty, about the age their father was when he died. They say it was hard growing up without him, but they add, "We were right in being in Vietnam, because to fight for someone else's freedom is never wrong. We in America have a responsiblity to the rest of the world to stop communism."

Donnie Mahowald now has a job driving snow-removal trucks for the city of Minneapolis. It is a part-time job but promises to evolve into permanent employment. His cancer is in remission. Nancy sees his old self emerging. "He has his self-respect back. That's why he got better." Nancy remains active in Agent Orange issues and has started writing a book about Donnie and Maurice and Vietnam. She is still angry, but slightly more patient. "Now when I get depressed or I am having a bad day, nothing can make me crabby. I just think, Donnie is working now, and then I feel better."

A television program about memorabilia left at the Vietnam Veterans Memorial mentioned Nancy's letter, and as a result, she and her brother started, hesitantly, to talk to each other about Vietnam and about Morris. Nancy also tracked down Sandy, Morris's widow.

When Nancy was in Washington, D.C., at the memorial, she touched Morris's name. She cried. And then she walked away. She was able to leave her guilt behind, but not her sense of the futility of the Vietnam War. "Those fifty-eight thousand names are overwhelming to me. It is overwhelming to me that they all died and I can't think of one good reason why they did."

Tropical Snowstorm

The dark girl at the bar cannot understand this soldier
    talk of white powder from the sky somewhere
"Snowballs, snowmen and skiing" mean no more to her
    than soldier photographs of last year's blizzard
So . . .

The bartender opens the old refrigerator,
    removes the beer,
unsheathes his combat knife,
    and scrapes a fistful of frost.
He tosses the crystals into the air,
    and as they fall, real slow-motion
    to the floor below,
The men stare into the girl's
    wide brown eyes
"I do not understand."

John, Art, we love you, come home
        William Barillas

SAMMY EDWARD KINNAMON

Specialist Four, 101st Service and Support Company,
U.S. Army Support Command, 1st Logistical Command
DECEMBER 8, 1947–FEBRUARY 26, 1969

SAM

I see you in pictures
I hear your name,
But I don't know you
And you, the same.

You were killed
Just two months
After I was born,
By something that is going on no more
That awful thing that was called,
The Vietnam War.

Many people tell me
You were a fine man,
And that you loved me so.
But deep in my heart
I'll really never know.

Now I'm grown
And I look a lot like you,
Who would have known
I would grow up to look like
Someone I never even knew.

———•———

CHRISTIE KINNAMON GARR doesn't know very much about the Vietnam War. "In history last year, there was a little part of it in our books, but it wasn't talked about very much," says the seventeen-year-old high school senior. "We just went through it." Her sense of the war that killed her father comes mainly from what people tell her. "From what I hear, we really didn't have to be there."

Christie is not bitter about Vietnam. In fact, she says, she doesn't know what to feel about it. But last Memorial Day, when she helped her grandfather put out flags on soldiers' graves, including her father's, that was important to her. "It's strange," she says. "I'll never know what he was really like."

What Sammy knew of his daughter came from a tape of her screams and squeals in the delivery room, played back over his cassette recorder in Vietnam; Christie's mother, Charlene, wanted Sam to hear the first sounds his daughter made. It was the closest they ever came. Christie was born the day after her father's twenty-first birthday; ten weeks later, he was killed when a rocket hit the supply jeep he was driving.

In the small town of Independence, Kansas, not much has changed in the nearly two decades since Sam Kinnamon's death. Families work hard; teenagers drink beer, cruise through hamlets like Elk City, Fredonia, and Cherryville, and go to dances on weekends. Life is not much different from what it was long ago when Charlene, then seven, met Sam, who was playing the trumpet while she danced in a recital. They dated throughout high school, went steady, broke up, and dated again. In her yearbook, Charlene saved Sam an entire page, but all he wrote to her was "Good luck next year to a real nice girl . . . Love ya, Sammy."

But the summer after she graduated from high school they were married. There was a big wedding in the First Christian Church, followed by a weekend honeymoon in nearby Coffeyville. They started off with more hope than money, but Sam had a job, and they were happy. To the newlyweds in their tiny first apartment, the future looked as predictable and secure as their past.

But in 1968, less than a year after their wedding, Sam's reserve unit was abruptly called up for duty. Charlene wanted to go with him when he was sent to Georgia for basic training, but she was two months pregnant and her doctor recommended she stay put. Sam was shipped off to war along with his best friend, Clay, and Charlene's brother; Sammy Kinnamon was the only one who didn't come back to Independence.

Christie and her mother don't talk about Sam very much. Charlene married a local man in the construction business, John Garr, when Christie was small and Garr is the man Christie thinks of as her dad. She has a younger sister.

Still, the enigma of her biological father billows like a puff of smoke over Christie's life. She can only wonder and daydream about Sam because those who knew him have shared very little with her about what he was like. When she was younger, she never really probed and no one really offered. She doesn't even remember how she found out about Sam; she just became aware that she had an extra set of grandparents.

Poetry is where Christie works out, or at least expresses, the things in life that puzzle her. She wrote her first poem after a friend was killed in a farming accident. Christie says she has to feel something before she starts a poem. "I can't write just about anything," she says. "I can't write if there's nothing there." A friend once asked her to write a poem about a police officer in town who committed suicide, but she couldn't because she didn't know the man.

In the spring of 1985, Christie learned that a friend's mother was going to the Vietnam Veterans Memorial; she had heard that people left things there, and she asked if a poem she had written to Sam could be placed by his name. A year later, Christie got a call from a television producer, who wanted to include the poem in a Memorial Day program about memorabilia left at the wall. Christie was flabbergasted, and her mother was excited too. They talked a little bit more about Sam, and her mother told Christie that she missed him at times. And after the television program appeared, townspeople approached her to say they knew Sam, she had never realized how many people remembered her father. "I've learned a little more," Christie says now, and she has compiled an informal list in her mind of the things she knows about him.

Sam played right tackle on the football team and was in a band called the Pendulums. He got okay grades, worked hard, enjoyed practical jokes, and was an Eagle Scout. He was looking forward to coming home and seeing her. In a big box of his things, kept upstairs in her house, she has found his Purple Heart, dog tags, and a childhood book called *When I Grow Up*, as well as an odd assortment of Buddhas that he wore on a chain around his neck. The tape of her birth is in the box, too, as are the official letters of condolence Charlene received from President Nixon and General Westmoreland. The more Christie finds out, the more she wants to know. "How am I like him?" she asks. "I want to know everything. About him, his attitudes. I'll always wonder. Everybody will give me answers, but it will never be like him being here. I'll really never know firsthand."

June 12, 1986

I was carried off the hill in a stretcher to a low spot and medivaced to a ship somewhere off Vietnam's coast. It is only now that I am able to visit this austere shrine and ask my unanswerable question: Who else died at Ashau Valley that June day in 1969? A part of me did. And I have only this wall to talk to. I miss that part of me that is gone and those who were there that day as only they remember the part of me I left behind. The part of me that I lost that day is now given to the wall in hopes to erase the hurt and be a benefit to all.

John Reynolds
LCpl, USMC
Omaha, Nebraska
3rd Marine Division

To: Thomas John McMahon (1947–1967)

I remember: the first time you placed your arms around me,
enveloping me with a security unknown until that day.

I remember: the times we shared in adolescent laughter, and the
devilish grin that transformed your face from serious to
magical, always making me smile.

I remember: tiny maple leaves in Spring, bursting forth to greet a
new season, very much like us—new, green, innocent,
yet eager to experience the newness surrounding them.

I remember: the little things that made the mundane the marvelous;
the smell of your after-shave, the texture of your hand in
mine, and how the very sight of you brightened my day
beyond belief.

I remember: the twinkle of your jade green eyes, the touch of your
hand against my neck, and the cascading sensations
caused by your kiss.

I remember: all those memories and moments of happiness, those days
of you and me, those days, so many yester-years ago.

I remember: for you have entrenched your memory in my soul for
always for I shall always remember you!

Love,
SMCF

EDWARD C. ZIMMERMAN, JR.

Lance Corporal, Company F, 2nd Battalion,
4th Marine Regiment, 3rd Marine Division
AUGUST 9, 1946–JUNE 25, 1966

November 21, 1984

Dear Eddie,

This is really a strange letter, for you have been dead for almost 19 years. As a matter of fact, you have been gone from my life almost as long as you were with me. I guess that's what makes this note so strange.

This is the second letter I have written to you since 1966. Your death has affected me more recently than ever before. I wish I knew why. I know I miss you a lot, but your memory will never fade. You would be as proud of your country as I am proud of you. Just two years ago, America built a memorial to all of you who served and died in Vietnam. Your name even made it in an issue of Time *magazine! Yes, I wish you were alive. You would be very proud of your little brother.*

I remember fondly, when you came home from boot camp with a stripe. There you were, all primped, standing tall in your dress blues. You looked great. I do feel bad that you had to go and I didn't. Mom took your dying really hard. I guess I did too.

I wish you could have met my son, Joel. He is a really special person. Of course, he's kind of mad (sort of) right now. I'm separated from my wife, and I know he would rather have me at home. I love Joel like a son and a brother. Sometimes I find myself taking on the role you played with me when Joel and I are together. Most of the time, I never think of myself as a father, but as a brother to my son. I know that sounds strange, but I think I'm trying to be all things to him. He has no brothers and I like being his friend. I just hope he doesn't hate me as he grows up because I left home. I don't think he will.

I usually come here to touch your name a couple of times a year. Last year, when I brought my class to D.C., I teach 5th grade, I could not stop crying. I didn't expect that to happen, but the emotions were too strong to keep down. I don't even know why I cried. It still pains me to know that you died so young. Mom has your silver star at home—yes—you won the nation's second highest honor. You saved a fellow soldier's life after your patrol was hit in an ambush. As you pulled him to safety you were struck with a number of rounds from automatic weapons. You crazy fool. Anyway, I'm alright and doing fine. You are a good person and a good Marine. I will love you always.

Your younger brother
Grant

———————•———————

"MY BROTHER was the person I looked up to," Grant Zimmerman says. "I wanted to be like him. He always seemed to know what he was doing. He was cool. He was the oldest boy in our part of the neighborhood who was willing to play with us."

Their parents were divorced when the boys were in the sixth and ninth grades. After that, "We kind of took care of each other," Grant says. In the summer, Grant and Eddie planted a vegetable garden; cucumbers were easy to grow, and the boys liked them because they came up fast. They hunted for praying mantises, catching as many as they could, seeing who got the most; they loved to watch them eat bugs. On Friday nights they never missed *The Twilight Zone*. "You just turned out the lights in the house and got scared out of your pants."

Eddie told Grant about sex and taught his kid brother how to make model cars. "We beat up on each other a lot," Grant chuckles. They were boys, not saints.

More people in their hometown of Muncie, Indiana, carried lunch buckets than briefcases, and plenty turned out when John Wayne movies played in town. It was a community staunchly in step with patriotism and "My country, right or wrong." "Military service was not only okay, it was preferred," says Grant. "There were lots of kids who didn't go on to school." Eddie was one of them. He left high school a few credits short of his diploma, and his mother signed the papers enabling him to enter the Marine Corps when he was just seventeen. It was 1964, the month before the Gulf of Tonkin incident. "Honestly, at that time, Vietnam was not in anyone's mind in Muncie, Indiana," Grant remembers. "You might hear about it occasionally, but it was so far away."

When Eddie came home on leave from boot camp, Grant was dazzled by his dress blue uniform. "I had gotten much bigger while Eddie was away," he says. "I had about three inches and about thirty pounds on him. But we became friends again real fast." Each day, the brothers went down to the soda shop together for cheeseburgers and shakes, strawberry for Eddie, chocolate for Grant. Then Eddie went off to Vietnam.

There didn't seem to be much to worry about at first. "It was almost as if he was away at camp," Grant says. "We would send him presweetened Kool-Aid to put in his canteen." But Grant began to sense a change in Eddie's letters home. "In the beginning, they were like 'Gosh, I'm here, and the country looks like this and this.' But the longer he stayed, the sparser and sparser they became. He didn't come right out and say it, but reading between the lines you got the feeling he was thinking, I really don't want to be in Vietnam and we really don't know what we are doing here."

Eddie survived ten months in Vietnam. "He was in a small patrol. There was a man out at point. They got ambushed, got caught in a cross fire, and the point man went down," says Grant. "The point man was the only one hit in the ambush, but he was still alive, and my brother went after him, picked him up, and dragged him back; he made it about halfway when he got hit himself. Both of them ended up dying."

Grant remembers the moment he found out. He was sixteen years old. "It was right around eleven o'clock in the morning, a Wednesday. I remember a car pulling up, Father Zeigler's car, a black Ford Falcon. He and my mother and the recruiting officer walked into the house—my mother was in tears. I knew the minute they walked in what had happened. My mother said, 'Eddie's dead,' and I ran out of the house. I went over to my best buddy's house; he could always get his father's car. We put the top down and drove out to the swimming hole and we spent the afternoon there, kind of ignoring it."

Grant had never wanted to surpass his brother, just to emulate him. Eddie quit the Boy Scouts; Grant dropped out, too. Eddie started smoking, so Grant started smoking. Eddie ditched classes, ditto Grant. It had seemed harmless. But after Eddie's death he wondered sometimes, did he want to die too? As he approached his nineteenth birthday, Grant knew that turning twenty was one thing his brother never did. The conflicts grew.

Grant finished high school and began wandering the hippie circuit from San Francisco to Woodstock. Yet despite growing doubts, he obeyed the law and registered for the draft in 1968. The war was wrong, Grant thought, but he was willing to fight "because the idea of government and democracy transcends those who lead it. We were not fighting for LBJ but for America and what it is." That's what Eddie fought for, Grant believes, and why he did not die in vain. "He honestly believed that he was doing what he should be doing."

But Grant is still bitter about what happened. "I am angry that he died when it was needless," he says. "I'm angry that those young persons were manipulated by the kings and queens of American politics.

"I'm not angry at the North Vietnamese or the Viet Cong who killed Eddie. I am more angry with, first, the South Vietnamese government, and secondly, with our government—Bob McNamara, Mr. JFK, Tricky Dicky, Mr. Johnson. It was ridiculous, absolutely ridiculous, for the thing to turn out the way it did. There was no reason it had to happen."

Today, Grant Zimmerman teaches fifth grade in Chapel Hill, North Carolina. He is divorced and has a son, Joel, with whom he first visited the Vietnam wall in 1982 at its dedication. "It was an awesome display of emotion that I don't think I was ready to handle at that time," says Grant. "There were a whole lot of people, and I think I got more involved with watching them express their feelings than expressing my own."

About a year later, Grant took his students on a class trip to the capital. They stood in front of Eddie's panel, and Grant talked about his brother. Suddenly, "I just broke down. I could not stop crying. It was really embarrassing with all these kids milling back and forth saying 'Mr. Zimmerman's crying, Mr. Zimmerman's crying.' "

Grant wrote to his brother just before Thanksgiving, 1984. He had no plans that year, no place to go, so he thought of visiting Washington, D.C. "I had friends up there, so I thought I could go up, see them, and say hello to Eddie. There was almost something that commanded me to go to the memorial. What's the old sixties word, 'vibration'? Well, that aura seems to exist around Eddie's name. No matter who's around you, it seems to be possible to communicate through those engraved names."

He pauses and thinks for a moment, then says, "The wall is really heaven. The country went through its own purgatory, and then those names were resurrected. They seem to grow out of the ground to me. They've all been sent to heaven. Everything is okay with them. They don't need to be hidden anymore. They've been pushed out of the ground for all of us to see."

June 86

To the Sporting Crew:

Well, it's been a long time since we've talked. I haven't seen you guys for a long long time—yet it seems to me that we're still together.

There are a lot of things I want to tell you guys—What happened—

After a lot of you bought the farm in summer, we continued to work the ridge lines and vallies from the Ashau to the DMZ, then went to the Laotian border.

I got hit couple times on January 6th. I was getting so fucking short I couldn't even hold a long conversation, but shit, you know how that goes. Those of us that were there did a helluva job keeping my ass alive. I still have both legs and can walk—not real fast—but what the hell. It seems in that valley we hit the 79th and 33rd NVA regiments —no wonder there were so goddamn many gooks running around.

I went back to Ft. Benning when I got out of the hospital. I saw Millbury in Japan. He was doing okay. Got into some shit for grabbing at a Donut Dollie. Then worked at Benning as an instructor. Many times I thought about you guys. It's hard to teach people what it was going to be like to take an infantry unit into combat. I got out in July '73. No shit, you guys would have freaked, the lifer just packed it in and left. 1st Lt. Infantry retired.

Most U.S. combat units left Nam in '73. In '74 the gooks came down the trail like big dogs. The South Vietnamese did okay and retook most of the country. Then in '75 they came again without U.S. support. It was all over. NVA still own it.

You guys are on a wall in D.C. It's an okay thing. It seems that somehow you are there. I've seen a couple of the guys since, but not many. Grif stayed for a few days last summer. I think we'd still be close if—

Saw Kim before they shipped us to Japan. She said you guys were Number 1. I don't know what happened to her. I guess she'd be about 30 now.

Saw Colonel Greene at Benning about a year later. He said "You know, I was in France, Germany, Korea and did three trips to Nam and never saw a better outfit than your Foot Cavalry—Sporting Crew."

Was in an airport a couple years ago. This guy is staring at me. He says "Chickenman, 34—" I said, "Roger that, Brass Balls 7." Brass Balls was clearly the best fuckin' medevac pilot in the world. We drank, talked and at the end we just cried.

Shitheads that were going to school at 4 fucking F say "beaucoup." Can you imagine that? I never say beaucoup.

People don't really understand. It's like the bush—when it was over, shit grew back and it was like we never were there, life went on —overall that was the best thing that could have happened. I don't say much, unless I trust them and they're cool. I think you guys would approve.

A Nam vet is in the Tomb of the Unknown Soldier and the 101st Airborne built a monument paid for by the alumni association. On it are names like Lam Son 719, Bong Ap, Ripcord, Hamburger Hill, Ashau.

No shit, the division ended up leading the league in kills and wilkie badges. We also took the most KIA, WIA.

They make dumb movies about the war—one guy wrote a book about 13th Valley—Texas Star. He didn't say but think he was 3/506 when they came up with us. Vets are sorta odd. At first, it was like some bum trip and never happened. Now they have parades and shit Guess time does that.

Doc—	*remember wrapping those bandages around my head that night? I told you it was my legs. Ha Ha only a few face scars that hair used to cover which tells you something you're missing in the aging process. Thanks, Doc, you are the best.*
Motown—	*Still like hockey, think of your ass when I go—don't skate anymore. Wings haven't done shit since then. Next year—Detroit is still there, not on fire.*
Wildman—	*Never did find your Donut Dollie. Fuck. She probably married some candy ass Air Force pilot. Bet she misses you!*
Freddie—	*I'd love to have some of your hot chocolate again. Nothing like it in the world. Wonder what you could have done with milk?*

Like to blow a Kool and talk about getting laid and then sit in the rain in an ambush til it got light enough for more chocolate.

Little Pete— *went to Seneca Falls for you—nice town—missed the ladies you said I'd find.*

Jimbo— *I take at least one hot shower a day. You're right, it's the second best thing. Sometimes I take two or three, try to remember to stay in a few minutes for you per our agreement.*

Berries— *I don't know. Kids are about the same. They invented a thing called Vietnam syndrome. So we're a little more careful about letting go the balloon.*

Soulman— *Temptations are still the best. You could go to school anyplace now. Fuck, they probably would even let you have a job.*

Bill— *What in the fuck did you go back up there for?? I wish I knew why, why Goddamn it, why!!?*

Allie— *World was like we thought—ice cream, whisky and shopping malls. Nice, clean, great, soft, getting over. This wall—I visited it in '83. It was dark and raining. Sound familiar? Damn it, was hard to walk down there, I was freaking. It's like you're there. Someday I'll go back and we can sit and talk. I hate the first week in June, late August and December the worst of times. Remember October, the best of times.*

The hardest thing is thinking. I remember the good. I remember the bad. Sometimes I laugh, sometimes I cry.

The worst thing is I tend to measure people by you guys and that's one fucking hard standard test. Fuck them.

When I'm happy, I think you share it and when I'm down I think you guys would be pissed. You know I loved you guys and I miss you terribly. We were tight. I wish it all turned out better—what did Dannie say? Nobody lives forever.

Can't think of you guys as angels. More like Valhalla, drinking beer, pissing foam, counting the days 'til we go home. Sometimes I sit in the dark and smoke—I see you in the smoke not like ghosts, but sitting calm—waiting to move out.

Life goes on—mostly good, sometimes bad, and there seems to be a hole where part of my heart used to be. (Doc would probably bandage my head.) I have trouble liking people and I'm afraid to like them too much.

I'd like to see combat one more time with you guys—feel the rush and the high. I feel responsible for each of you—could we, should we have done something different?

The world has changed—

No draft

Music is different

No race riots

Schools are integrated

Cities aren't burning

Economy keeps going to hell—jobs sometimes are hard to find

Gas is over $1 a gallon

The U.S. is still the best place to live

It seems that part of me is still there with you. Sometimes I wake up in the night—look for my weapon and get ready to go on watch or do commie checks. Sometimes you just daydream and hear a weapon fire or someone scream—then you realize you're here, not there.

People ask if it was worth it? No one really knows. Would we do it again? Hell yes, don't ask why. We were the best infantry company in the fucking world.

In the MASH unit the main man came down from Division to see Buckwheat, Sarge, Bozo, and me. He pinned medals on my goddamn pillow and said you were the best ass kickers in the 101st Airborne— thought the SOB was going to kiss us.

I went to this deal with my boss—A guy wrote a book about Bloods—at the end they asked Viet vets to stand up—I did—I did for all of us—people clapped—what the fuck—I think they meant it— wish you were there—maybe you were.

I feel better writing this—remember June 6? Why don't you shitheads ever write?

> *Miss you guys*
> *Currahee!*
> *Lt.*

Acknowledgments

This book could not have been written without the dedicated research and assistance of John Campbell, a Vietnam vet from Glassboro, New Jersey. I met him because he had left a letter at the wall, and when I interviewed him and heard the story of how he had traced the parents of one of his buddies, I asked him if he would like to help find people for this book. His research has been a blessing and his enthusiasm and devotion to the book something for which I have more gratitude than words. Everything that is fine about a Vietnam vet, he is. His wife, Betsy Campbell, helped us tremendously. Her kindness and sensitivity added to the spirit of this book.

My agent, Kristine Dahl, had faith in and enthusiasm for this book from the very beginning. I rely on her intelligence, her perseverance, and her humor, which never fails.

Random House has been a superb ally. My editor, David Rosenthal, has an uncanny sense of what works and what doesn't, and his commitment to this book never wavered. His assistant, Julie Grau, kept the momentum of the book going by keeping track of absolutely everything. Virginia Avery, the copy editor, treated the manuscript with care and competence that strengthened every page. Carole Lowenstein gracefully coordinated the artwork and layout.

Jan Scruggs and Maya Ying Lin, whose combined visions created the Vietnam Veterans Memorial, gave both wisdom and feeling to this book. Sandie Fauriol and Jack Wheeler of the Center for the Study of the Vietnam Generation could always be counted on for worthwhile insight and guidance.

Earl Kittleman of the National Park Service was eager to do what he could to help me. Ken Gochenour and Joe Westermeyer, park rangers at the memorial, always managed to find answers to my questions or know the people who would. Steve Alemar, who was the lead ranger at the memorial for nearly two years, understands its dynamics as well as anyone I've found and happily shared his experiences with me. Pegi Donovan, Bill Schorndorf, John Bender, Frank Bosch, Ira Hamburg, and Marty Kaplan are several of the volunteers who give so unselfishly of their time and compassion at the memorial. They all increased my understanding of what it means to visit and work there, and I wish to thank them for that.

David Guynes is the curator at MARS, where the thousands of items in the Vietnam collection are stored. His devotion to his work is surpassed only by his intelligence and skill in figuring out how to tackle such an overwhelming job. With the barest of resources he runs a thorough and meticulous operation. Kim Robinson and Jeanne Southard are two of his bright young assistants who became my friends.

Buddie Moore and Billie Loftin in the Hardin County Courthouse in Kountze, Texas; David Payne, the barber in Sour Lake; along with Rev. Glenn Dromgoole, the Baptist minister, and Diane Rutledge, the librarian, in nearby Silsbee, all helped find the family of Eddie Lynn Lancaster.

Don Kirst and his wife, Mary, in St. Paul, Minnesota, were an absolute godsend to this book. Don painstakingly pursued countless leads that, after dead-ending in Canada, eventually got going and led to Carole Page in Eugene, Oregon. Tom Buttry, the librarian at Hopkins High School; John Tesar, the retired band director; and Steve Hauer, an alumnus, contributed pieces of the puzzle.

In Minneapolis, Jim and Marilyn Rosenbaum and their daughters, Alexandra, Catherine, and Victoria, supported this book wholeheartedly from the very beginning.

Delores Smith, a librarian in Toledo, Ohio, and Rev. John Dyer of the Augsburg Lutheran Church suggested clues that located Yvonne Sherman.

Although they are not related, Ann Daugherty proved to be the crucial link in tracking Chad Daugherty in York, Pennsylvania.

Ben and Bette Smith in Missoula, Montana, diligently tried to provide information that would lead to the author of a letter we believe was written to their son, Gary M. Smith. Joan Smith, also of Missoula, provided invaluable assistance. Several of his buddies also joined in the search: Bob Dedlow, Kennewick, Washington; Gary Steinhart, West Lafayette, Indiana; Bob Hartwick, Salisbury, Missouri; and David Farmer, Streamwood, Illinois.

Gerald Goist of Mesa, Arizona, and Charles Moman of Gardendale, Alabama, were pivotal in tracing the families of Rudy Valenzuela and Dan Neely.

William Granlund, the high school principal in Gaylord, Michigan, and his wife, Jean, were the bridge to Jean Strickler and Georgia Respecki. My aunt, Harriet Palmer, also helped with research in Michigan.

Skip Hutton and Paul Rappl in Orchard Park, New York, added information about their three classmates who died in Vietnam: Gary Townsend, Billy Mason, and Doug Henning.

John Slonaker of the U.S. Army History Institute in Carlisle Barracks, Pennsylvania, thoroughly and patiently pursued many inquiries connected with research for this book, as did Janet Kinzer, a librarian at the Arlington, Virginia, public library. Dan Crawford of the Marine Corps Historical Center in Washington, D.C., was an asset, as was John Wilson of the U.S. Army Center of Military History.

Doreen Spelts of Doylestown, Pennsylvania, generously shared with me her knowledge about the eight nurses killed in the war.

Also in Pennsylvania, Carl Hamberger cooperated with me fully in Camp Hill. Bob and Mary Ebers in Shoreham, New York, added to the scope of this book by sharing their story with me. Gwen Derenne and Jean Crabtree at Wheatland High School in Wheatland, California, also helped.

John Del Vecchio of Newtown, Connecticut, suggested useful contacts with the 101st Airborne Division. Other Screaming Eagles who were happy to help were Charles Hawkins, Oakton, Virginia; Chip Collins, Lebanon, Virginia; Ray Blackman, Valparaiso, Nebraska; and John Mihalko, Whippany, New Jersey. Rod Souvers of Fort Washington, Maryland, helped steer us through the National Archives.

Larry Wagner, a Vietnam vet in Turnersville, New Jersey, willingly did anything he could to help this book. Wes Caton, a vet in Manassas, Virginia; Rick Rogers in Wichita, Kansas; and Mike Massaro in Williamstown, New Jersey, all spoke candidly to me of their experiences in Vietnam, which broadened my understanding of the trauma some veterans have endured. Dr. Steve Singer, a therapist who works with vets in Coatesville, Pennsylvania, also gave me guidance. Duery Felton, in Washington, D.C., added to my awareness of the problems of minority vets.

Paul Scanlon published the first thing I ever wrote when I submitted it to him at *Rolling Stone*. Thirteen years later he assigned the magazine piece for *GQ* which led to this book. He is a gifted editor and a dear friend.

Dr. F. Forrester Church of All Souls Church in Manhattan encouraged me by saying simply that this was a book that had to be done. He was one of the very first to appreciate the spirituality of this material.

My octogenarian pal, Helen Foster, has a faith in me that defies any logic but is very sustaining. Her wisdom and counsel have mattered deeply to me over the years. Virginia Jayne Bird is the one person I can always count on to understand. Erika Hoefler's love and devotion to my daughter make it possible for me to work with a clear conscience. Myrtaris James enhances my family with her genuine cheerfulness and goodness. Mary Browne helps figure out the answers when I get stuck and Tad Bartimus always makes me laugh. My friend Frank Mariano has, I know, been with me in spirit.

Helen and Joanne Palmer, my mother and sister, have kept me going with a love that knows no bounds. My husband, Stephen Geer, was supportive and patiently endured a wife who was distracted, traveling, or getting up at five in the morning to write. Eve Geer, my mother-in-law, has encouraged me in my work, as have Gail and Kate Palmer with their kindness. My father and brother, Bud and Mark Palmer, have shaped the way I look at the world. But it is my daughter, Sabrina, for whom I am most thankful because her gaiety, goodness, and love give meaning to my life.

If you have left something at the Vietnam Veterans Memorial and wish to provide further information about it please write to:

David Guynes, Curator
MARS
P.O. Box 283
Lanham, Md. 20706

If you recognize someone in this book as a friend of yours and wish to contact his family, please write care of:

Shrapnel in the Heart
Random House
201 East 50th Street
New York, N.Y. 10022

ABOUT THE AUTHOR

LAURA PALMER has lived and worked as a journalist in Saigon, Paris, Washington, D.C., New York, and Los Angeles. She grew up in Evanston, Illinois, and was graduated from Oberlin College. She is married and lives in Manhattan and Edgartown, Massachusetts.